# THE LAST MINORITY
# WHO WILL IT BE?

BY

MENDEL D. HILL

**DORRANCE**
PUBLISHING CO
EST. 1920
PITTSBURGH, PENNSYLVANIA 15238

Dorrance Publishing Co
585 Alpha Drive
Pittsburgh, PA 15238
Visit our website at *www.dorrancebookstore.com*

ISBN: 978-1-6453-0072-4
eISBN: 978-1-6453-0180-6

# TABLE OF CONTENTS

# PROLOGUE

## 1961 - SPRING IN AMERICA

John and Mendel, both 21-year-old inquisitive black youths, were about to experience similar confrontations with the unyielding social structure existing in America. John, born near Troy, AL, was within a month of obtaining his Bachelor's Degree from the American Baptist Theology (ABT) college in Nashville, TN. While attending ABT, John had been trained in the nonviolent civil disobedience philosophy of his mentor Dr. James Lawson. Further, he was an active participant in challenging the segregation policies of local stores and movie theaters. Mendel, born near Buffalo, NY, had attended college for two years in Pennsylvania, joined the Army, and sought to pursue a civilian career like his selected mentor Supreme Court Justice Oliver Wendell Holmes, Jr.

## STUDENT JOHN LEWIS, NASHVILLE, TN

In early April, James Farmer, Chairman of the Congress of Racial Equality (CORE), invited John to be one of a number of Freedom Riders chosen to participate in an interstate bus demonstration throughout the South testing the 1946 Supreme Court ruling against segregation. The trip would begin in May. As the bus trip departed from Washington, DC, John disembarked not long after the start to attend a job interview hoping to rejoin the group somewhere further south.

As fate would have it, the bus was viciously attacked in Anniston, AL, burning the bus and harming many riders. John had not joined the bus at that point. Fearing further harm to the riders, Farmer cancelled the trip supported by the NAACP and Martin Luther King, Jr.

Upon returning to Nashville, within a few days, John and his Nashville friends were organizing a replacement trip scheduled and controlled by his own Nashville Student Group and not CORE. The trip would proceed from Nashville to New Orleans going through cities like Birmingham and Montgomery. In advising against the trip, Farmer used the words "suicide" or "massacre."

The departing group of 10 students consisted of six black males (Harbour, Bull, Brooks, Barbee, Carson, Lewis); two black females (Collins, Burke); one white male (Zwerg); and one white female (McCollum). Each was required to write a last will. The group was attacked at the Montgomery Bus Station by a vicious mob of hundreds of armed men, women, and children. Both John and the white male, Jim Zwerg, sustained severe head wounds, that required their hospitalization. Zerg was beaten so badly that he remained for two weeks and was returned to Wisconsin by his family.

*John Lewis and Jim Zwerg, bloody from Montgomery Bus Station Attack - 1961*

*Officers Candidate School - Welcoming Sign - 1961*

## PRIVATE MENDEL HILL, FT. SILL, OK

Duffle Bag in hand, I was about to enter the Army's Artillery Officer's Candidate School (OCS) in April 1961. I was met at the OCS gate by four Upper Class (Lower Class, two months; Middle Class, two months; Upper Class, two months) white members who had designated themselves a welcoming committee.

"What are you doing here solider?" one asked in a heavy southern accent.

"I have Orders to report here today," I responded.

Almost in unison, their response was, "Niggers don't graduate from here, so why don't you sign this Resignation Form and return to your old unit!"

When I refused to sign, all hell broke loose. The four escorted me to the OCS compound and subjected me to about two hours of physical and verbal harassment that included screaming the word "nigger" in my face over and over and hundreds of push-ups and sit-ups and forced runs until I would collapse. Eventually, I assume I had passed out since, when I came to my senses, the four were gone and the crumbled, unsigned form lay on the ground next to me.

The intensity of this harassment lasted for four more months because after completing the two months of Lower Class, I was required, if I wanted to stay in OCS, to repeat two more months of Lower Class over again. Even though I was passing academically, I was rated low in leadership. Without hesitation, I accepted another two months of Lower Class, marking my total time gaining my 2nd Lieutenant bars as eight months in lieu of six months.

*Lt. Mendel Hill - OCS Graduate - 1961*

## THE CULTURE BLANKET

While both John and I were experiencing similar stressful experiences in the spring of 1961, there was a far more personal similarity that would support both throughout our whole lives. We were both wrapped in our culture blanket, which provided each of us a personal strength that would not have existed without it.

# INTRODUCTION

Someday I expect an acquaintance to approach me with an apology something like this: "I apologize for my actions. I guess my human nature caused me to do it."

I have come to understand that, while historically new, our nation is definable, is a melting pot of many languages, cultures, and religions. Europeans, Africans, Asians, Middle Easterners, Native Americans, and Hispanic migrants from the remaining Americas have successfully mingled to create a wonderful and powerful nation. While we are blessed with abundant natural resources and arable land, it is the immigrants and their cultures that have been the most important asset in the development of our nation. No modern nation has ever been created by such a diverse human platform. It is our burden and our blessing.

The question before us is how did this historical reality happen, and why have I concluded that the combination of immigrants and their cultures exceeds the other contributing factors such as availability of national resources, stable political environment or temperate climates. This book will first review the historical, evolutionary paradigms from which our United States society has evolved. From that baseline, we will build our case for the importance of immigration and culture in our world tomorrow.

There are certain realities that have existed since humans evolved that impact our today's society. I have identified three PERMANENT REALI-

TIES that each of us faces today from time immemorial. They are here to stay, and you must deal with them. Period! I have also identified two SOCIAL REALITIES that impact every life, but are under the individuals control to manage.

# THE THREE PERMANENT REALITIES

### ◆ HUMAN INSTINCTS

During my research, I wondered how a southern family could prepare a picnic lunch, go to a prearranged location with other families, and watch a lynching of a Black American. First impression—unforgivable. Second impression—blame it on Human Nature: fear; anger; jealousy; envy, rivalry; curiosity; affection are all an instinct in all of us. In a search, for understanding, I will not use the simplified word racist in this book. Human instincts are at play in all of our social discourses.

### ◆ HIERARCHICAL SOCIETY

In his book *Sapiens*, Yural Noah Harari gives an insightful analysis of human development thousands of years ago following the Agricultural Revolution. He cites the manner by which these evolving humans "organized themselves in mass-cooperation networks (societies) when they lacked the biological instincts necessary to sustain such networks." His conclusion is that the developed networks (societies) divided people into "make believe" hierarchies of privilege, workers, and slaves. The Hammurabi Codes established three levels of society (the top, middle, slaves). Aristotle discussed "slave nature and free nature." Hindus created a caste system stating that Gods created each cast. In 1776, the U.S. Congress created its own network groupings with white males at the top leaving women and slaves as inferior.

I offer Harari's theory in an attempt to stimulate thought, to stimulate the reader's search for understanding our society. Today, we do live in a hierarchical society. Does it matter how it started? It is important to note that almost all societies throughout the world are hierarchical. The question is, however, if we accept the hierarchical order as a natural phenomenon, must we still account for the human instincts that operate within this imposed order?

### ◆ MIGRATION

Immigration is a central issue confronting the United States today. Immigration, however, is just one subset of the natural phenomena of human migration which commenced out of Africa almost two million years ago. There are thousands of examples of human migration to all parts of the world for economic, social, political or environmental reasons. In my mind, when immigration is debated, I place it into a more historical context which is the natural animal (human) drive to migrate. Migration is natural; immigration with its laws and cultural biases is not.

# THE TWO SOCIAL REALITIES

### ◆ ECONOMIC STRUCTURE

This book will address the importance of <u>economics</u> in our society and the role it has played and will continue to play in our society. It is important that the reader appreciate that the economic structure is permanent, determined to maintain its controlling powers, yet adaptable enough to adjust to societal changes (e.g., the end of slavery) while maintaining continued control without missing a beat. Sharecropping and Black Codes in the South replaced slavery. One can complain that the Oligarch's command of money is unfair, or you can become one as many have.

### ◆ THE POWER OF IMMIGRANT CULTURES

You will also be appraised of the perfect antidote (CULTURE) to the whims of the economic/monied juggernaut—The Four Economic Pillars. As Peter Drucker says, "culture eats policies for breakfast." Many first-hand personal experiences are included that support that conclusion. One caveat is that the culture must be strong. In the absence of a strong culture, the individuals are left to their own personal drive.

# 1

# IMMIGRATION:
## THE DYNAMIC ELEMENT

## UNEXPECTED RENDEZVOUS

It was late evening on April 17, 2017, and I was reading a front page article in the *Washington Post* entitled "In Iowa, the meaning of a life, death and another cup of coffee." Eighty-year-old Russell Paulson had gathered with his regular friends at the Quik Mark in Kiron, Iowa, population 229 (nine Mexicans and 220 white residents). At 6:30 AM, they were drinking their coffee and discussing the death of Walt Miller, a member of their coffee group the night before. Further in the conversations, someone brought up the words spoken by another local inhabitant Steve King, who is also a member of the United Sates House of Representatives. King had recently stated that "cultural suicide by democratic transformation was occurring because we can't restore our civilization with somebody else's babies."

The group members knew that King was expressing a sentiment that they all understood. Essentially, the sentiment was anchored by three obvious truths… that their white population was shrinking, that towns like theirs were vanishing, and that the only population growth in their area was being driven by immigrants from Mexico and Central America working at a pork processing plant nearby.

After reading the article, I stepped outside of our condo in the Washington, DC suburbs for some night air. There, in the dark, I was confronted by a pizza delivery driver looking for his delivery address. As I directed him to his intended address, I noted his age (at least 60) and his very heavy accent (possibly Middle Eastern). So within a very short span of time, I had been treated to an unexpected rendezvous between two competing realities facing our nation. The first being the historical, national obsession with the maintenance of white supremacy and the white culture. The second being the inexorable striving of other than white immigrants seeking a better life.

## IMMIGRATION HISTORY

The United Sates is an immigrant nation, and that fact defines us. Except for the indigenous Native Americans, all persons living within our borders are immigrants or descendants of immigrants. Further, except for the Spanish, Portuguese, French, and Dutch failed efforts, our nation is an extension of the Anglo-Saxon emerging nation-state of England and its culture.

The challenges facing the English colonialists back in the 16th century were enormous. England had evolved from a Nordic peoples (Celts, Scandinavians, Germans, Dutch, French) that had taken 1,000 years of invasion and warfare to become an all-white nation. These English colonists, however, were faced with a virgin continent stretching from ocean to ocean that would be required to produce wealth for England initially and subsequently for the United States itself. History tells us that the principal wealth producing resources (prior to the industrial revolution) were initially the Free Labor of Indentured Servants and Slaves followed by the waves of Irish, Southern and Eastern European almost-white immigrants. These immigrant waves were closely followed by immigrants of "color" being waves of Asian, Mexicans, Middle Eastern, and Africans.

The United States, therefore, has been faced with two competing, inexorable realities. The first being the wealth generating economic need for immigrant labor described above. The second being the fixed desire to maintain a white culture with all the social and economic prerogatives associated with white privilege. As the English culture took centuries to develop, the United States culture cannot yet be defined since titanic, evolutionary skin color trends are occurring not only in the United States but in the Americas and the world. These trends and the shrinking of this world through instant communication and travel have led to a yet evolving definition of "white" that will be less associated with Western European skin color and more with whoever can meet the white privileged standard of social, educational and economic superiority. When one individual or one class meets the standard, neither skin color, race, nor national origin will matter.

## IMMIGRATION LAWS

During the colonial period prior to the formation of the United States, small numbers of "white" immigrants (English, Irish Protestants, Germans, educated Jews, Scandinavians) settled in the colonies. In 1790, however, the first Congress passed the Naturalization Act, which limited naturalization (the process by which a non-citizen may acquire citizenship) to immigrants who were "free white persons." The Act did not place restrictions on immigration. Over the subsequent 200 years, National and State laws and national perceptions of non-white immigrants imposed periodic restriction on immigration. The Chinese Exclusion Act of 1882 and the Immigration Act of 1924 restricted immigration of Chinese and Southern/Eastern Europeans respectively. In 1888, President Cleveland maintained that Chinese were ignorant, could not assimilate, and would be dangerous to our welfare. On another level and in an effort to thwart the land acquisition successes of Japanese immigrants, in 1913 the California Legislation enacted the Alien Land Law which, prohibited Japanese non-citizens from owning land. You will see from the following three family histories that the Chinese, Japanese, and Mexican immigrants adapted quite well to the United Sates. First, however, we will address migration.

# MIGRATION

When one addresses the current discussions and policies of immigration, it would offer better insights into the issue if one is cognizant of the larger issue migration. Our species, homo sapiens, have migrated to every part of the earth starting thousands of years ago. Humans migrate! With the advent of nations and borders, migrate is replaced by emigrate (to leave one country) and immigrate (to arrive at a new country). The United States, as well as other countries, developed immigration laws exerting control. Through these laws, decisions are made for who may migrate, how many may migrate or what skin color may migrate as immigrants.

# IMMIGRATION STORIES

### ◆ LISA LAW - MY PARENT'S STORY
Lisa Law is a Brown University graduate with a Master's Degree from Harvard University. Lisa also has a nonprofit corporation that provides education assistance to youths in Ghana, West Africa.

*My parents lived in China during Mao's Cultural Revolution (1966-1976), which was a sociopolitical movement set into motion by Mao Zedong, the Chairman of the Communist Party of China, to spread and solidify the communist ideology throughout the country. Mao called on the nation's youth to purge the "im-*

*pure" element of Chinese society and revive the revolutionary spirit that led to victory in the civil war 20 years earlier, which resulted in the formation of the People's Republic of China. During this chaotic period, the Party closed all schools and forcibly displaced a large segment of the population, including anyone deemed as "intellectuals" and "subversive" to the Party. Families and friends turned against each other as everyone was labeled suspicious until they proved their loyalty to the Party. Millions of youth, including my parents, were forcibly transferred to do manual labor in the country side so that they uphold the values of communism by experiencing the life of true proletariats. The actions of the Communist Party tore the country apart, undermined the development of the country, and wasted the potential of an entire generation of Chinese youth.*

*My parents, who were not able to complete high school, did not see any opportunities for them living under a communist dictatorship, decided that they needed to escape the country. They traveled by foot through the mountains in the nighttime and slept in cemeteries to avoid being caught. They made an inflatable float to help them across the East China Sea to reach Macau. Their float capsized a few times, and they lost friends in the treacherous journey. Although they were caught and jailed three times, they made it successfully to Macau, where they were smuggled to a fish boat to Hong Kong in 1975. They lived in Hong Kong for three years, applied for political asylum and immigrated as refugees to the US in 1978. They settled into NYC's Chinatown. My mother was seven months pregnant with my brother, who was born in April 1978. I came two and a half years later.*

*I remember very vividly the tenement building in Chinatown where we grew up. My father worked various jobs to support the family—from washing dishes, to being a janitor, to being a waiter. My mother stayed at home to raise my brother and I and took care of my grandparents who later immigrated to the US. My fa-*

*ther later learned enough English to attain a real estate license and earned enough to move the family out of our cramped tenement to a bigger house in Brooklyn. Because of my parents,, who were the first to land on US soil, I have 40-plus relatives who live in NYC now, all of whom subsequently immigrated to the US. Both sets of my grandparents had the opportunity to come to the US and live their rest of their lives in a land that provided the entire family more resources to pursue a more successful life than they had growing up.*

*Because of my parents, the thought of wasted potential has driven me to help individuals maximize their resources through education to lead productive lives. I know that if my parents had the same opportunities and resources that I have, the path to accomplishing their dreams would have been unhindered. I often envision my father as a university professor, and my mother as a nutritionist and swimming instructor. Instead, their youth was spent in turmoil as they were forced to toil in the countryside. However, in the US, my parents continued to pursue their interest—my mom used to swim every day and still reads the Chinese newspaper voraciously to inform the family of nutritional facts, my father, a great orator, joined the community board to represent the Chinese in our neighborhood in Brooklyn. If equipped with a formal education, I have no doubt that my parents could have reached their full potential.*

*Therefore, my parents instilled in me a boundless appreciation for education and encouraged me to look beyond the borders of Chinatown, where I was born and raised. Ever proud to be American citizens, my parents always reminded my brother and I their story of making it to the US. They don't ever want us, or the next generation, to forget and take living in the US for granted. They always ask that no matter what we do in life, they hope that we contribute back to society when pursuing success and personal fulfillment.*

### ◆ JOSE MARTINEZ - MY PARENT'S STORY

Jose is the son of Juan Martinez who immigrated to the United States with his family of eight from Mexico in 1924. Each child was required to obtain work at the age of 12 to provide financial support to the family. At the age of 12, Juan began working for a Japanese family that grew fruits and vegetables on their family farm near San Jose, CA. Jose states that his father, Juan, never attended school after the age of 12, but learned to be fluent in English and Japanese nonetheless. Over the years, Juan became an accepted member of the Japanese family. The family was Interned in 1942, and the family turned the business responsibility of the farm over to Juan. During their absence of almost four years, Juan was successful in expanding the business while providing long distance support to his adopted family. Upon the Japanese family's return, Juan assumed ownership of the expanded business he had created and paid the previous owners handsomely for the business.

### ◆ THE BESSHO FAMILY - MICHI'S JOURNAL EXCERPT

*Gentaro Bessho, our father, came to America in 1906 from Osaka, Japan. His ship was to land in San Francisco, but SF had an earthquake and a big fire which made it unsafe for the ship to land. They had to go to Vancouver, Canada. Father worked his way down to Seattle, WA, where he probably worked in the apple orchard or on the railroad as many did at that time. Mother, Saku Tauiguchi Bessho, came to America about two years later with their daughter, Masako, who was about three years old. Mother did some housework and told us about the woman of the house running her fingers over the furniture that she had cleaned. She must have learned to cook there for she made stew and various other dishes for us. When Masako was five years old, she became ill probably with influenza which was spreading at that time and died. Her death influenced them to go south to the Los Angeles area, where it would be warmer. They settled in Montebello where many of their friends* lived. Masako was buried in Seattle's oldest cemetery in town. Michi visited her grave when she went to Japanese American Citizen League Convention held in Seattle in 1936. A family friend, Mr. Okuda, took me there. I'm sure Setsu was with me when I visited again. Setsu was born in Seattle. Masako had a small white cross located far back on the left side of the cemetery.

Mother was from Obamu F., west of Kyoto on the coast of Japan. Father was from Osaka where his family had a general store. One of things Father did was make coral beads which was made into string of beads. He brought several with him, which mother gave to some friends and to us girls of the family. The Bessho family must have had a large living quarters because Mother's brother lived with them when he went to school in the city. Mother's brother recommended Father marrying his sister, so they did. Father had a younger brother whose picture I have seen, but we did not learn too much about the family.

Setsu was the only one born in Seattle, all the rest were born in Montebello. There were many families from Fukui in Montebello, where the Busshos came. Their close friends were Tobinagas, Sugetas, Yamamotos, etc., and they helped each other adjust to the new environment. They went into flower business. First growing small flowers such as violets, sweet peas, etc., that could be put in baskets. They didn't have cars then, so Father rode a bike to the train and carried the flowers into Los Angeles to sell. We lived in a wooden house with a kitchen, dining area, large bedrooms, and a place to prepare flowers. The bath was in a separate building Japanese style where you wash first and go in a hot tub. The water was heated by firewood. The bath was connected to a large room used for sleeping by the worker and the children as we outgrew the main bedrooms. The sweet potato cooked in the bath fire was a treat for us.

We had to go the distance of the second building to the outhouse. Mother had a washing machine outside in those days. We *were all born in this house which was about a block away from the new house. They had bought four and a half acres on Beverly Blvd. I had Dr. Trewella at birth, but all the rest had midwifes. Mrs. Ofarie, who lived on Soto Street in LA, a few houses south of First Street. There was a three-car garage separate from the house. The family car was a Hudson with jump seats, a second hand from their good friend, the Hirais, who had a nursery in Hollywood. The piano also came from the Hirais which the Hakanos now have. Their daughter took classes at USC. Father also had a truck by this time. Father had a horse on the property to do work in the field There was buggy also.*

## REFLECTIONS

These three stories reflect the enormous strength, hard work, and adaptive skills that immigrants bring. They also reflect an energy, a cultural centricity, and a can-do attitude that has enhanced and contributed to our United States society. Immigration has definitely made the United States the most dynamic society in the world. Based just on these three demonstrations and the others that follow, there must be a continued alert to recognize the important contributions that immigration brings. Today, the old prejudices continue to be exerted against immigration. In order to thwart the immigration of new contributors, the Trump Administration has labeled Mexicans as rapists and "bad hombres," and labeled Muslim immigrants as "dangerous terrorists," has proposed building a 2,000 mile wall along our Southern border with Mexico to keep the "rapists" out, and has proposed deporting millions of undocumented Hispanics who perform the services that no other previous immigrant will stoop to.

Just as today, every wave of immigration has been resisted. The potato famine in the 1840s in Ireland encouraged two million Irish Catholics to our shores. When they arrived in the eastern cities, they were treated worse than the Free Negroes. They provided important "cheap labor" in farming and railroad building. Chinese immigrants came to the west coast near San Francisco in response to the gold rush started in 1848 and initially provided "cheap labor" in agriculture fields, mining, and railroad building. Within a few years, the Chinese Exclusion Act was passed. This Act, however, opened the door for Japanese immigration until the Immigration Act of 1924 cut off immigration by Japanese. A much larger wave of Eastern and Southern Europeans totaling in millions started arriving in the 1880s. These arrivals were not considered "white" by the Western Europe standards. They were utilized as cheap labor in their employment opportunities.

# 2

# CULTURE:
## THE UNFORESEEN EQUALIZER

This chapter is not an in-depth analysis of culture. The focus is on the similarities (Anthropologists refer to it as "The Comparative Approach") in the adaptive skills of the various immigration groups as they strive for assimilation. In fact, immigrant cultural strengths many times impose their will in circumstances where normal economic considerations would hold sway. As our immigrant population defines the United States, the "culture blanket" brought by these immigrants guarantees a successful and sustainable life of opportunity for all. The power of culture is exemplified in one concise statement spoken by the noted management guru, Dr. Peter Drucker, which is "Culture eats policy for breakfast."

It should be noted that each culture group came to our country with their own unique culture blanket. So it seems normal that each group's success relied on their own set of cultural strengths. Based on my research, the cultural strengths of the groups have a consistency. While there are many elements to each cultural blanket, I have selected six elements that commonly apply among the various groups.

The first element is COLLECTIVISM, where working together is paramount and where the interests of the individual are generally subordinate to the group. A revealing example of collectivism is provided in the first eight pages of the Bessho Family Journal kept by Michi Imai that begins with the grandfather Gentaro's arrival in 1906. Her hand writing and descriptive details offer a unique insight. The whole journal highlights the heartaches, the progress despite social and political barriers (e.g. the four years of Internment), the total absence of negative interpretation of life's events, and the smooth transition to a financially secure and educated class.

The second and third elements are FAMILY SUPPORT and GRIT respectively. As with the collectivism, these two attributes are not developed in the new environment but are brought from the departed homeland. From the moment of arrival, the demands imposed by the existing society would overwhelm without support from family or ethnic friends and/or without the self-developed confidence of the immigrant.

The fourth attribute EDUCATION EMPHASIS, at times, comes with a particular immigrant group (e.g. Asian) and, if not, should become a developed priority. Interesting comment from my second-generation Korean friend bemoans what she considers the over emphasis on multiple degrees dating back to the 16th and 17th centuries. I have found that recent immigrants from Africa and the Middle East also place heavy emphasis on education.

The fifth and sixth attributes, POLITICAL POWER and FINANCIAL STRENGTH, have proven to be necessary cultural assets. For example, the Irish Catholic culture of secret societies, unionism and social bonding helped them exert political power twice in the 18th century. Likewise, the Jewish cultural strengths of financial emphasis and educational pursuit and family closeness (e.g., Jewish Mothers, smile) certainly helped in their assimilation.

# CULTURE STORIES

### ◆ JAPANESE CULTURE

Gentaro Bessho immigrated to the United Sates (through a temporary landing in Vancouver, Canada) by ship in 1906 from Osaka, Japan. His grandson, Stuart Imai, hired me as an employee of the California Institute of

*442 Regimental Combat Team*
*World War II - Japanese Decorated Unit*

Technology in 1983. Stuart's parents, Tom and Michi, married on June 25, 1941, and Stuart was born in 1946, a year after his parents returned home to the Los Angeles area after four years of internment imposed by President Roosevelt's February 19, 1942, Executive Order 9066. As a result, 120,000 Japanese (70,000 being citizens) from California, Oregon, and Washington were relocated to Internment Camps inland.

Japanese immigration began in the 1880s as the Chinese Exclusion Act of 1882 took effect. These immigrants assumed many of the farming duties along the west coast, particularly in California, Oregon, and Idaho, even with a penchant for acquiring or leasing the farm acreage. By 1913, the industrious Japanese immigrant communities prospered through cultural strengths of collectivism, education, and land acquisition focus. They were so successful that in 1913 California enacted the Alien Land Law, which prohibited non-citizens from owning land. Later, Congress enacted the 1924 Immigration Act that prevented almost all immigration for three decades. This law supported the 1922 Supreme Court decision that naturalized citizenship was extended to "white persons" and persons of African descent. Despite these barriers, Japanese Americans prospered by combining resources through social organizations, savings and loan banks, and social assistance groups.

It is important to note some unique cultural strengths of Japanese. The first is "Gaman," which briefly put is "don't complain." The journal never once complained about the four years of internment away from their homes, businesses, and schools. Another strength is "duty." WWII's most decorated Regimental Combat Team, the 442nd, was comprised of Japanese personnel. The unit was the recipient of 21 Medals of Honor and 9,486 Purple Hearts. For emphasis, these soldiers fought and died for our country while their parents, brothers, and sisters were subjected to unconstitutional bias.

Did you know that while the 120,000 west coast Japanese were interned, 150,000 Japanese living and working in Hawaii were not interned. These Japanese were needed for the Hawaiian economy to function. Economics Trumped Prejudice!


◆ **IRISH CULTURE**

"The law does not suppose any such person to exist as an Irish Roman Catholic."

That quote is said to have been uttered by two separate judicial authorities under the Penal Code system imposed on Irish Catholics in Ireland. The Irish that immigrated to the United States prior to 1830 were primarily Protestants. Post-1830 and particularly during the Potato Famine years of the late 1840s, almost two million Irish Catholics arrived.

Noel Ignatiev, author of *Ignatiev - How the Irish Became White*, provides an excellent history of (1) the conditions in Ireland imposed on

Catholics, (2) their arrival status in the United States likened to "a nigger turned inside out," and (3) their ascendance to political power by the strengths within their culture. One of the strengths brought was a common religion, and a second strength brought was a tradition of labor organization and secret societies as one name Ribbonmen. These Irish workers labored as dock workers, coal diggers, railroad builders who were sufficiently organized to impose effective and sometimes violent strikes to gain concessions from businesses.

To fully understand how the Irish immigrants came into full flower as United Sates citizens and how they assimilated as a group, you have to appreciate the courage and wisdom displayed by what I call the PIVOT! In 1841, the Irish leader in Ireland, Daniel O'Connor, obtained 60,000 signatures for his political proposal that was sent to the American Irish Catholics. The message was that American Irish must support the abolition causes being pushed by northern politicians and churches. This proposal, based on the fact that Ireland prided itself for never allowing slavery on its soil, was soundly rejected by the Irish now living in America. Their position was that they are Americans and must bring their status above their nearest competitor… the Negro. For that reason, it is speculated that their Philadelphia vote for the southerner Democrat (Polk) won him the election in 1844.

Four decades later, the sophisticated application of their political power actually delivered the disputed 1876 presidential election to Rutherford B. Hayes. Samuel J. Tilden, a southern Democrat was actually leading in the Electoral College numbers, but some were disputed. The Speaker of the House, Irishman Randall, a Democrat, negotiated a settlement that gave the Republican Hayes the Presidency in exchange for Hayes withdrawal of Federal Troops from the South, thereby ending Reconstruction.

## ◆ JEWISH CULTURE

The first recorded Jewish immigrant arrived in James City, Virginia, in 1621 from France, and in 1669 the South Carolina colony supported religious tolerance through a charter that supported religious tolerance to Jews. In 1740, the English Parliament passed the Plantation Act that permitted Jews to be naturalized in the colony. In the 1840s to the 1850s, large numbers of liberal, educated German Jews immigrated, and with these numbers, negative stereotypes began to emerge. These Jews were Reform and Conservative Religious Jews. It is speculated that an early pivot (moving away from Orthodox) was made so that the Jewish immigrants could more easily be absorbed into the United States culture.

Before the 1880s, the Jewish immigrants had been assimilated rather easily into the United States population and been considered white. With the arrival of over 28 million from southern and eastern Europe, including Jews, the white establishment began to term the immigrants as "other than white" and warned about the Mongolic nature of the Nordic race. During these same years, however, Jewish businessmen began to assert their financial acumen and strength. Having been small businessmen earlier, they started investment banking on a national scale through Goldman Sachs, Solomon Leob and Jacob Schiff, and the Lehman Brothers. Adding a personal note, Edward Jasnow, a friend and work mate from NASA, is a product of a great grandfather who immigrated, escaping a Russian Revolution of 1905 and a mother from Hungary who immigrated in 1920. This is significant because both beat the 1924 Immigration Act that severely limited immigrants from eastern and southern Europe.

In her book, *How Jews Became White Folks*, Karen Brodkin identifies the central strengths of the Jewish culture… those being a culture that sticks together, hard work, education, and deferred gratification. She went on to elaborate that Jews did not just pull

themselves up by their own boot straps but that Jewish success is partially the product of powerful social barriers (e.g., the G.I. Bill, FHA, and VA Mortgages) removed for them and other whites when, at the same time, these support programs were not available to African-Americans.

Notwithstanding the obvious successes that Jewish immigrants enjoyed with the assistance of their cultural blanket and notwithstanding the history of Anti-Semitism of the United State society in general, one cannot ignore the abandonment of the 900 plus German Jews who sailed on the liner "St. Louis" in 1939. These immigrants seeking safety from the coming horrors of Nazi Germany were denied entry into the United States by our Congress and President Roosevelt. They were required to sail back to Germany, where many died. There was also a Congressional proposal, which was also turned down, to allow 20,000 German Jewish children to immigrate here. During this effort, the wife of the head of the U.S. Immigration Commission (also a Roosevelt) stated that "20,000 charming children would all too soon grow into 20,000 ugly adults."

The reason President Roosevelt would not issue an Executive Order allowing the 900 Jews residency in the United States was because he was seeking an unprecedented third presidential term in 1940. He chose not to risk his coming political success by supporting the Jewish retention.

# 3

# ORIGINS OF
# BLACK CULTURE

## INTRODUCTION

In my mind, the pursuit of civil liberty and civil rights has been a constant effort by all immigrant groups who came to our shores. For black immigrants, the pursuit can be separated into two phases. Individual or small group efforts were the hallmark from the time we reached our shores to the beginning of the modern civil rights era. Starting around 1940, new tactics were being employed by the black community and their white supporters.

> *Colonization dehumanizes the most civilized man; that colonial activity, colonial enterprise, colonial conquest, which is based on contempt for the native and justified by that contempt, inevitably tends to change him who undertakes it; that the colonizer, who in order to ease his conscience gets into the habit of seeing the other man as an animal, accustoms himself to treating him like an animal, and tends objectively to transform himself into an animal.*
>
> *Discourse on Colonialisms*
> *by Aime' Cesare (1955)*

## SLAVERY IN PERSPECTIVE

Let's put slavery into perspective though a historical lens. Slavery has existed for thousands of years throughout all of human history. In Rome, there was a five layer social structure: (1) Civil and Military Aristocracy, (2) Traders, (3) Artisans, (4) Peasants, and (5) Slaves. In the 15th and 16th centuries, Africa was ruled by powerful states (e.g., the Songhay Empire or the Asante) whose primary wealth came from gold near the today nations of Ghana and the Gold Coast. These people typically used gold to purchase slaves. The Asante rulers subjugated approximately 20,000 slaves to work the mines and to clear the forests for agriculture. With the arrival of the Portuguese in the 15th century, the powerful Africans assisted the Western Nations in gathering and shipping between 10-15 million slaves to the Americas. So even at the beginning, both Europeans and Africans used slave labor to enhance their economic interests. The Triangular Trade route between the home country, Africa and the Americas commenced around 1562 by an English sea captain. While at about the same time, the Spanish, in 1565, inaugurated a regular trade and slave route between Manila, in the Philippines, and Acapulco, Mexico.

## EARLY BLACK CULTURE

It has been over 150 years since slavery was abolished. It has also been this same period of time that the former slaves and their children have had the opportunity to develop a solid cultural base. At this point, I am proposing that we accept, as a fact, that a strong or even limited black culture did not exist at the outset of freedom. Up to that point the culture bomb had held sway.

> *The effect of the culture bomb is to annihilate a people's beliefs, their names, in their languages. in their environment, in their her-*

*itage of struggle, in their unity, in their capacities and ultimately in themselves. It makes them see their past as one wasteland of non achievement and it makes them want to distance themselves from that wasteland"*

*"Decolonising the Mind"*
*Ngugi wa Thiongo*

We can turn to more concrete actions by blacks. Leadership was evidenced by three black leaders during this period. The first was Frederick Douglas, born in 1818, who escaped slavery at the age of 20 and who became a leader of the Abolition movement until his death in 1895. Booker T. Washington, born as a slave in 1856, became the founder of the Tuskegee Institute in Alabama. Based on the financial support provided by rich whites, he became the leader of black Americans with his conciliatory speech in 1895 at the Atlanta Exposition. It was in this speech that he offered the Atlanta Compromise. "In all things that are purely social we can be as separate as the fingers, yet one as the hand of all things essential to mutual progress." In essence, social equality would not be sought by the black community. The counterweight to Washington was W.E.B. DuBois. Born in 1863 in Massachusetts. DuBois gained Bachelors and PHD degrees from Harvard University. In contrast to Washington, he demanded equal rights for blacks. In 1909, he participated in the founding of the National Association for the Advancement of Colored People (NAACP).

With careful reading of the books written by DuBois and Washington, we find that both recognized a social theory that DuBois called the Talented Tenth. The black masses were to be led by the educated black elite. To me, the implication was that the 90 percent of blacks neither had the intellect nor the social skills necessary in a free society. Similar thoughts pervade in our black culture today with the educated elite 40 percent having no connectivity with the bottom percent of blacks who remain under-employed, under-educated, and without hope.

# BLACK HEROES

*Buffalo Soldiers Company*

### ◆ UNKNOWN BLACK SOLDIER

Have you ever visited Fort Garland? I have! It is located in southern Colorado, in a huge, desolate flat plain a few miles above the New Mexico border. Garland is one of possibly 50 forts that black soldiers occupied stretching from the Mexican border to the Canadian border. In 1867, two infantry and two Calvary Regiments were established and sent to the western plains to suppress the Indian attacks on white settlers. In more than a hundred battles, the black soldiers were awarded 14 Medals of Honor for their bravery. Yes! We are talking about the Buffalo Soldiers who served from 1867 to about 1897.

*My dear Mother… Our troop has been very highly complimented and the Captain is the hero of the hour. Do not tell me about the colored troops there is not a troop in the U. S. Army that I would trust my life to as quickly as this K Troop of ours. I have seen them only once but it was in a place where a stampede would have meant massacre. The firing was at 200 yards… No men could have been more determined and cooler than these same darkies were… The wounded Corporal has had to have his leg cutoff, the ball that shattered it lodging in the other instep. This man rode seven miles without a groan... Such I have found the colored solider.*

*Letter, Camp of Troop K 10th Calvary, May 10, 1886*

### ◆ ROBERT SMALLS

Robert Smalls is a national hero (1) for commandeering a Confederate war ship out of Charleston Harbor in the dead of night in 1862 while he was a slave and (2) for achieving five terms as a United States Congressman after the Civil War. He and his slave shipmates sailed the ship out of the harbor and turned it over to the Northern ships blockading the harbor.

Robert Smalls is <u>my</u> hero because the above actions were not his primary goal. Those actions were simply opportunities that assisted him in reaching his primary goal of keeping his slave family (wife and two sons) intact. He could buy the family's freedom for $800. Even when he made $15 a day working at the shipyard, the sum of $14 was given to his owner. He knew he could never accumulate the necessary $800. Additionally, he had to be concerned that his owner could at any time, sell his family members piecemeal at any time.

Smalls had developed a careful plan to steal the ship with his family members on it. One evening, the Captain and all white crew members went to Charleston for the night. Smalls had arranged for his family and any crew member's family to meet along the shore. There he picked them up and proceeded through five check points before arriving out at sea. One agreement he had with his family due to the tremendous risks being undertaken was that if the escape didn't work, they should join hands, jump into the sea, and perish together.

### ◆ NATE TURNER (1800 - 1831)

Nate Turner was born a slave in Southampton County, VA, in 1800. He and about 70 armed fellow slaves attacked his master's family and about 15 other white farmers and families and killed about 60 people. Turner and his associates were caught and hanged by authorities. Turner's Rebellion in 1831 and Gabriel's Conspiracy Rebellion (a blacksmith slave near Richmond, VA) in 1800 were two incidents of over 200 similar slave revolts in U.S. history.

### ◆ SOJOURNER TRUTH (1797-1883) AND HARRIET TUBMAN (1822-1913)

They were great abolitionists and civil rights activists. Sojourner was a gifted public speaker who dedicated her life helping former slaves adapt to their new freedom. Harriet escaped slavery in 1849 from Dorchester County, MD. She then immediately returned to guide her immediate family members and dozens of other slaves to freedom. She also was an armed scout and spy for the U.S. Army during the Civil War. After the war, she established her home in Auburn, NY.

## FORWARD AND BACKWARD

The conclusion of the Civil War left a significant impact on the established social and economic norms. Human slavery was abolished. The northern states had gained control of federal policy taken from the southern states. The nation, in the midst of a devastating war, had expanded its rail connection from the east coast to California, avoiding the tough passage across Panama. The resulting industrialization would soon establish the nation as a major western nation-state like England and France. The child had become an adult!

Moving forward would present the nation, both north and south, with the conundrum of what to do with my ancestors, the former slaves and free blacks. How could this former economic sustaining resource of free labor be integrated into the new economy without serious disruption? The Four

Economic Pillars, acting in seamless coordination, implemented solutions over an 80-year period that met their goals. The solution (1) replace the "slave labor system" with the "share cropping business system" throughout the South, which returned the former slaves to slavery by another name (John Lewis' Family); and (2) employ the free blacks and millions of coming immigrants in cheap labor categories in the north working in company towns (Mendel Hill's Family). Whether north or south, Edgar Furniss' dictum of keeping laborers living "at the margins of subsistence" was achieved by the triumvirate after the war.

OK! So there was a successful macro-economic pivot executed by the Four Pillars from slave labor to cheap labor. The next question is: What impact has it had on John Lewis' life and mine? My conclusion is that it has been a major factor not only in our two lives but in all black lives since the 1860s. As I grew up in the north, my father worked for a cheap labor Tannery Factory, and my mother performed maid service for well-to-do whites, in addition to cleaning the town bank. As he grew up in the deep South, John Lewis' father was a Working-on-Half share cropper, and his mother either worked in the fields or hired herself out, as my mother did, performing maid service for the well-to-do.

Notwithstanding how economic actions affected the lives of my parents, grandparents, and myself and John, we can also review how they did it. I do not want the importance of their actions to be lost! The economic powers are alive and well today, and they remain poised to pivot through the next crisis for their own gain. Keep the poor... poor! The collaboration started when the federal government brought three Constitutional Amendments (13th, Abolish slavery; 14th, Citizenship; and 15th, Right to vote) and two Civil Rights Acts (equal protection and public accommodation). The Freedmen's Bureau was also formed to assist blacks with education and land. These federal laws were immediately countered throughout the South by State enforcement or restrictive "Black Codes" and "Jim Crow" practices. In effect, federal laws were completely trumped by new state laws and practices. Both the federal laws and the counter state laws were acceptable to the oligarchy.

*Company Tannery House*
*Hill Family*

*Elkland Tannery Strike*

*Father Manzo, Sr. - middle;*
*Grandfather Henry - on his*
*right*

It is at this point that the "100 year experience rule" should, in the least, demand a pivot by black organizations and activists. Maybe, just maybe, it will become obvious that continually striving for civil rights and civil liberties is the wrong objective. The old saying, fool me once - your fault; fool me twice - my fault! Now that my light bulb is on, I don't recall any other immigrant group striving for "RIGHTS." Damn! They strive for "ASSIMILATION!"

- The Civil Rights Act of 1964 - barred discrimination in employment and other areas.
- The Civil Rights Act of 1965 - outlawed discrimination in voting.
- Civil Rights Act of 1968 - barred discrimination in the sale or rental of housing.

Wasn't there similar legislation enacted exactly 100 years before?. The 13th Amendment abolished slavery and involuntary servitude. The 14th Amendment of 1868 required due process and equal protection under the law for all citizens. It also stipulated that the right to vote could not be denied by any state. The fact is that the 1860s laws did not improve the lives of black citizens for 100 years. The laws enacted in the 1960s produced similar, negative results regarding black citizens. Identical techniques at the state level negating both sets of laws were effectively employed. In essence, same positive laws, same negative results!

Here is a cursory review of the actions taken by civil rights supporters over the past 150 years:

(1) Institute legal challenges like Brown vs. Board of Education;
(2) March, as in 1963 on Washington and March across the Pettus Bridge in Selma, AL, in 1965;
(3) Voter registration drives in the hundreds including the famous Mississippi Summer Initiative by thousands of students;
(4) Reliance on black leaders, black ministers, black organizations like the NAACP; and
(5) Riots in Los Angeles and other cities.

These are the tools used by the black culture and their supporters to affect change. These attempts were worthy, were dangerous for the participants (even death), and sometimes reached their goals. They did not, however, seriously impact either the political or financial interests of the opposition. They were, no matter the frequency of use, a strategic failure! Chapter 6 identifies the Montgomery Bus Boycott as the major strategic effort in the black community to affect change.

There is another option available! The Irish Catholics, relying on their cultural strengths of secret societies and unions, participated in politics and gained national political power. The Japanese used collectivism, land acquisition and (my favorite) Gaman—do not complain. The Jewish immigrants used collectivism, education, and financial strength. While I may have missed it, I do not recall these immigrants using the techniques of my people, such as Marching; Protesting; Litigating; Rioting. They didn't have to! They had confidence in and they relied almost exclusively on their own cultural strengths to achieve their civil liberties. That option is available to us. Our black culture needs to PIVOT away from unsuccessful techniques and towards proven, successful techniques as the Irish Catholics and the poor women in Montgomery did.

# 4

# BLACKS ARE
# IMMIGRANTS

Black slaves were involuntary migrants starting around 1619. Blacks became free and gained citizenship in 1865. Blacks became immigrants symbolically around 1915 at the time of what is known as the Great Migration of 8 million escaping the horrible conditions in the south. In the north, and eventually the south, blacks could compete almost equally with the other arriving immigrants. Unlike the other immigrants, however, blacks lacked the strong cultural tools to effectively overcome the systemic barriers that contributed to what Isabel Wilkerson in her book, *The Warmth of Other Suns* described as "a silent pilgrimage" within our borders.

> *There were share croppers losing their settlements...Yard boys scared that a single gesture near the planter's wife would leave him hanging from an oak tree. They were all stuck in a caste system as hard and unyielding as the red Georgia clays, and they each had a decision before them. In this, they were not unlike anyone who ever longed to cross the Atlantic or the Rio Grande.*

I am a grandson of both sets of grandparents who chose to escape the holocaust environment in South Carolina and Tennessee respectively around 1915. There were over 4,000 lynchings of black men and women and

*Alice (Phoebe) Hill—grandmother*

*The prince, Mendel Hill, age 4*

*The Prince, Manzo Hill, Jr. age 6, older brother*

*The Hill family vacation*
*Empire State Building, NY, NY, 1949*

*Darne and Manzo Hill, Sr.*
*Dining in New York City*

countless rapes of black women by white men. The southern environment was as horrendous for them as the immigrants who escaped Mao and Hitler. This migration was assisted by northern industrialists who sent recruiting agents south seeking black workers for their factories' WWI production goals. There was great resistance to these northern efforts by the southern states who wanted to retain their "cheap labor" resources. Some southern States, especially Georgia, placed felony charges against suspected agents. Black passengers on trains heading north were searched, detained, and jailed often.

Alice and Henry Hill migrated from St. George, SC, to Olean, NY, as maids and servants to the rich. Alcenia and Thomas Edwards migrated from Memphis, TN, to Olean, NY, in employment of the railroads. My father, Manzo Hill, and Mother, Darne Hill, both labored in low income jobs but ensured that my brother and I were provided the family and educational support to successfully compete in the white society. There was heavy emphasis on grades obtained in school and on weekly music lessons. We vacationed every summer in New York City, visiting the Empire State Building, Yankee Stadium, shopping on 5th Avenue and the center of the Black Urban World Harlem and the Theresa Hotel. While living in a white world, each summer, I saw black achievers like Jackie Robinson, Sugar Ray Robinson, Minister and Congressman Adam Clayton Powell at his Baptist Church.

The Great Migration gave millions of black boys and girls the ability to perform daily comparative analysis with the dominant white society. We competed every day in academics, in sports, in music, and in common social adjustment. That opportunity was never allowed in the caste system in the south. But if we look carefully, if we see these north/south differences through a cultural eyeglass, strong culture bridges the gap between my experiences and those of my hero from the south, John Lewis.

While we were growing up in two socially different environments, John and I had two identical strong cultural traits supporting us… strong family support and determined support for education. In his book *Walking in the Wind*, John discusses circumstances that were important to him. One circumstance was the Summer trip to Buffalo, NY, with his Uncle Otis Carter in 1951. Uncle Otis planned this special trip for John as he was aware of John's potential. They traveled to another uncle's home, where John saw blacks and whites living and working together. As an aside, my parents took my brother and me on a similar car trip in1951, but we were traveling from New York to Memphis, TN, to visit great-grandmother Reed. John wrote about the special precautions taken as they traversed Alabama, Tennessee, and Kentucky. I similarly recall the special precautions we took as we drove south into Kentucky and Tennessee. My brother and myself were warned to be courteous and even afraid of southern whites... which we followed to the letter!

What I have gathered is that the Great Migration advantages provided to the black children in the north, like myself, did not exceed the advantages of the black children who remained in the south, when each was wrapped in strong culture. Conversely, those black children in both north and south not afforded strong cultural support were not going to be able to beat the social barriers.

We cannot leave the story of the Great Migration without assessing the root causes of what I would call a significant social explosion. Isabel Wilkerson dramatically described the cast system facing southern blacks after the civil war as "...as hard and unyielding as the red Georgia clays..." That system included the obvious culprits of intimidation, Jim Crow, sharecropping, lynchings, and rapes. There is, however, another rarely mentioned contributing factor to the continued maintenance of the cast system until the time of the Migration. That factor is the mutually supportive, symbiotic relationship that developed between the new black leadership and the white society, particularly the churches. While debatable, I offer the ominous similarity of intent of the two entities to manage (black leaders) or control (white community) the black masses exiting slavery.

Two significant black leaders were W. E. B. DuBois and Booker T. Washington. While their positions modified over time, neither leader had faith in the ability of their black brothers and sisters to competitively exist in the dominate white society. Through this period, the concept of the Talented Tenth came into being. The black Talented Tenth would be the leaders of the black community, would receive the educational benefits offered by the white community and would manage the uplifting of the uneducated 90 percent.

On the other hand, the northern Baptists and Methodists starting with the Civil War through the next 50 years established over 50 institutions of higher learning for blacks. In fact, the American Baptist Home Mission Society (ABHMS) established 26 institutions throughout the south. Through these efforts we notice a merging of the Talented Tenth concept between the whites and the black leaders. The American Baptist Quarterly publication in 1993 addressed their concept and importance of the black Talented Tenth to the benefit of the white population. In that article, the Baptist T. J. Morgan proposed the idea that a highly educated, black elite Talented Tenth would form a protective buffer between the "uneducated demagogues" (poor blacks) and the white community. He envisioned a "colored American Yankee" that could intervene with the 90 percent when they may attempt insurrection against their white oppressors.

The relationship symbiosis was complete. Black leaders could manage their people in the manner proposed by Booker T. Washington in his "Atlanta Speech" as socially isolated through the educated Talented Tenth. This "unholy alliance" has had a lasting influence on our black culture. The class divide persisted as evidenced in the makeup of the Montgomery, AL, black community at the time of the Montgomery Bus Boycott discussed later.

There are continuing consequences, even today, of the acceptance of the Talented Tenth thought imbedded into our black culture. Those of us blacks who have expanded the Talented Tenth to an estimated 40 percent through expanding educational opportunities, for one, offer little assistance to blacks existing precariously in our ghettos. The continued, frightful circumstances at play in our cities like Chicago or Baltimore with black-on-black crime are not part of my black middle-class environment. I see daily examples of the slaughter in the newscasts when they may be within a mile or two of my protected location. Can a culture advance when a majority are left behind by their brothers and sisters lucky enough or educated enough to have escaped?

# 5

# THE MONTGOMERY BUS BOYCOTT

*"Not since the First Battle of the Marne has the taxi been put to as good use as it has this last week in Montgomery. However, the spirit animating our Negro citizens as they ride these taxis or walk… One feels that history is being made in Montgomery these days."*

As she observed the empty city buses rolling through the streets during the first week of the boycott, Juliette Morgan, a white librarian, posted this warning to the white community in a letter to the *Montgomery Advertiser*, a local newspaper. Yes! History was being made. More significant, however, is that this historical event frames an accurate picture of the struggle for civil liberty and civil rights faced by each and every immigrant culture arriving on our shores. The picture further reflects the strengths or weaknesses of a culture, reflects the intensity of the external forces aligned against, and identifies the cultural complexities that can, in themselves, determine success or failure.

The roots of the boycott were planted many years earlier in both the person of a little girl named Rosa and in the accumulating anger of thousands of the working black women who had been for years physically abused, humiliated, and arrested while riding on the segregated Montgomery Bus System. Further, unlike the transportation options available to their upper class sisters and brothers who owned cars, these working women had to rely almost exclusively on the bus system for transportation to work or shopping. Juliette's and my conclusions are based on the following observations.

1. The boycott was supported from the bottom up when thousands of black working women, assigned to the lower class, enthusiastically took up the call to boycott the buses, walk to work or catch a ride for a period of 381 days regardless of the weather.

2. Unexpected collective support from the upper- and middle-class blacks was provided through the provision of over 200 of their personal cars into a car pool network for the walking women.

3. The boycott targeted the financial interests of the white community establishing the worth of financial confrontation.

4. The evidence supports the fact that the boycott was supported by the whole black community including men and women, rich and poor. What tends to be missing in other civil rights initiatives, however, is the fact that women managed the key elements by deciding to boycott by alerting the community to the boycott and by assuming management responsibility for the day-to-day operations over the period of a year.

It is my opinion, supported by evidence provided throughout this book, that the MONTGOMERY BUS BOYCOTT was the only civil rights action taken on a significant scale by and for the black community to achieve the desired result. Comparatively, the 1963 March on Washington, the Thurgood Marshall success in the Supreme Court's Brown vs. Board of Education decision, the inner city riots of the 1960s and the combined Civil Rights Acts and Voting Rights Acts of the 1860s and 1960s have proven to be marginally successful, if at all.

Thus, the efficacy of any civil rights movement or action must be considered prior to the commencement of that action. Actions taken that do not consider the political or economic counter measures to follow will either have no success or moderate success. The boycott met its desired results. I cannot identify any other protest actions or legal actions that met the boycott's efficacy.

*The Marching Women of the Montgomery Bus Boycott*

## MONTGOMERY BLACK SOCIETY

Before addressing the details of the boycott, we should take a peek at the social structure of the black Montgomery community. It was a stratified social
structure common in the south made up of (1) influential ministers and the
well to do, (2) an educated middle class of teachers and small business entities, and (3) an uneducated lower class of maids, cooks, and service people.
It is estimated that only seven out of 100 in the lower class held a high school
diploma. It is also important to note that one of the influential ministers was
24-year-old Martin Luther King, Jr. This stratification is brought home by
two bus incidents involving black women passengers who were arrested for
refusing to give up their seat on a city bus. The first was Claudette Colvin,
who was unmarried and pregnant. The second was Mary Lou Smith, who
lived in the poor section of town where loud music was played and whose
father was an alcoholic. Each woman sought assistance from the black
Montgomery Improvement Association (MIA), which consisted primarily of
black upper class male leaders and was headed by E.D. Nixon, Ralph Aber-
nathy, and Dr. King. The assistance request was denied due to the low social
standing of both young women. The black women's political council (WPC)
headed by a Jo Ann Robinson, who taught at Alabama State College, was
not happy with the MIA rejection of the two young ladies.

## ROSA PARKS

On December 1, 1955, Rosa Parks, the civil rights activist, boarded that bus
in order to start the confrontation that did ensue. She knew, in her heart,
that she was the quality offender that the black leadership would support.
Rosa was raised by her grandparents; and her grandfather, Sylvester Edwards, was a major influence in her life. As a little girl huddled next to
Sylvester one night she watched him prepare for a deadly confrontation with
the Ku Klux Klan (KKK) with his double barreled shot gun on his lap. He

told her that he surely would get one of them, if they entered his home before they got him. Rosa relates that she was very excited and wanted to see the gun fired. Sylvester had always counseled Rosa never to be afraid of whites. Rosa eventually married Raymond Park, who was a barber, and assumed her career as a seamstress. Both Rosa and Raymond became active in civil rights, and Rosa joined the local chapter of the NAACP.

I offer one more confirmation, from an unlikely source, supporting the historic nature of the Montgomery Bus Boycott. While teaching at a Methodist missionary in India, James Lawson was creating such a disturbing noise from his room that a colleague came to inquire. There, he found Lawson dancing and shouting at the top of his lungs. On entering the room, Lawson pointed to an article in the local newspaper stating that Negroes by the thousands were boycotting the segregated bus system in a United States city. Lawson stated to the colleague, "This was the beginning. This was what he had been dreaming about, what he had gone to prison for, what he had come halfway around the world to find at its source...."

*Ms. Rosa Parks—being booked—1955*

Reverend Lawson's story is reserved for the discussions in Chapter 7, but his influence had an impact on this section. As a member of CORE in his youth, he became an advocate for nonviolence in the resistance to racism. In 1955, he was introduced to Martin Luther King, Jr., who had also embraced the Gandhi principles of nonviolence. King urged Lawson to come south from Ohio and help. Lawson moved to Nashville and became the nonviolent mentor to John Lewis and his Nashville Student Movement

## OBSERVATION

Cultural strength can produce both dramatic and decisive results on the political and social fabric of the United States. The cultural strength referenced here is the influence of black women in the black culture. Two circumstances that both occurred in the state of Alabama offer confirmation.

In the first circumstance, while the black men of the Montgomery Improvement Association (MIA) in 1955 and 1956 received the credit for the successful boycott, it was the black women like Jo Ann Robinson and the maids who kept walking for 381 days who produced the stunning victory. Compromise negotiations between the bus company management and the MIA were conducted through the boycott and would have resulted in some form of continued segregation. The black women of Montgomery, led by JoAnn Robinson, a teacher at Alabama State University, however, would only accept a total cessation of the segregationist practices. Statements by the walking women captured in Danielle McGuire's book, *At the Dark End of the Street*, confirm their resolve. "I ain't 'bout to get on dem buses... I'll walk 20 miles 'fo I ride 'em, I'll crawl on my knees 'fo I get... on dem buses."

Sixty odd years after the boycott, the same culture strength of energized black women was exhibited in supporting the election of a Democratic Senator in Alabama in 2017. It has been observed that a key component of the victory can be attributed to the voting power of black women. It is also interesting that unlike the boycott perceptions, black women voters were recognized to the exclusion of the black male contributions.

# 6

# THE MODERN
# CIVIL RIGHTS ERA

## INTRODUCTION

The previous chapter on the Montgomery, AL black social structure is a fitting introduction to the Modern Civil Rights Era. What is more telling in that chapter is the fact that the central strength of the black culture rests with the love and determined strength of women. Working black women brought the bus boycott to a successful conclusion. "At The Dark End Of The Street", a book authored by Danielle L. McGuire provides a more than thorough history of slavery and civil rights from the black woman's perspective. Her narrative has been an important contributor to this book and should be a must read for interested Americans. This chapter covers the era through a series of personal experiences starting with a revisit to Mendel and John's adult experiences (Northern Boy; Southern Boy) and concluding with individual experiences highlighting the era.

In my mind, the pursuit of liberty, rights, and opportunity have been a constant effort by all immigrant groups who came to our shores. For black immigrants, the pursuit can be separated into two phases. Individual or small group efforts were the hallmark from the time we reached our shores to the beginning of the modern civil rights era. Starting around

1940, new tactics were being employed by the black community and their white supporters. Black soldiers returning home from WWII were determined to secure their civil rights. Black college students and their white supporters (The Youth Quake) took the lead in attacking the existing standards of social injustice at lunch counters, movie theaters and voter suppression. Even more significant was the new tactic of nonviolent confrontation on a massive scale implemented by new leaders like Dr. King and John Lewis.

The Modern Civil Rights Era started out as a continuation of the old leadership style and tactics. Over time, however, the leaders evolved to a different type and background and the tactics became more confrontational versus legal. Ministerial leadership has given way to a more bicultural/political leaders, and the movement tactics are dictated by young black and white activists as opposed to mature leaders and organizations. Evidence of this milestone change in leadership and tactics is in the Interstate Busing confrontation in the early 1960s.

Civil Rights organizations were the instigators of the Freedom Riders tactics until the Anniston, GA, and Birmingham, AL, white violence riots either burned the buses and/or viciously attacked the Freedom Riders. The Federal Government and the involved Civil Rights organizations cancelled the busing plans due to the danger to the riders. They even described future rides would be "suicidal" for the riders. Notwithstanding the instructions and the dangers, the Nashville Student Group chose to ignore these orders, chose to assume leadership and chose to proceed into the mouth of danger no matter the personal costs. They rode the buses! They absorbed the horrendous beatings. Some survived! Some were killed! With these actions, a new leadership was born and the nonviolent protest philosophy was installed as the new tactic.

## NORTHERN BOY; SOUTHERN BOY REVISITED

We return to the lives of John and Mendel as their lives progressed beyond the Spring of 1961. We will start with their early years and the personal confidences gained from the culture blankets that embraced them.

### ◆ MENDEL HILL

I always knew I was special, and that feeling is still with me today. My first five years were spent in my father's parents' house in Olean, NY, with my father, mother, and older brother. It was a big, orderly home, managed by Grandmother Alice in a nice neighborhood with green lawns and streets made of bricks. Alice would provide moderate spankings when deserved to the older kids, but would grab my hand in hers, slap her own hand, and give me that look... of love. I would also be taken across town to Grandmother Alcenia's home, where my mother's younger brothers and sisters resided, nine in all. Alcenia always had delicious biscuits coming out of the oven, but the real treat for me was being hugged and kissed by my four beautiful aunts (Fannie, Helene, Jean, and Carol)

When I was five, we moved and established residence in Elkland, PA, which was 50 miles away from Olean. Elkland was a company town that supported the largest sole leather factory in the world. My father, Manzo, and grandfather, Henry, both worked there. Most of the homes were built at company expense, and workers would rent them. We lived on the hill with seven black families called Little Africa. Down the slope was Little Italy, where the Italians with their grapevines lived. Down by the river was Frog Town, where the eastern Europeans lived. Downtown had the Tannery Store, some small businesses, the schools, and the managers. At school, I was the only black in my class from 1st to 12th grade. Socially, one growing up incident left me proud of my blackness, while the second incident was a youthful reminder that black skin would be held against you.

I was invited to my classmate Bobby Rupar's birthday party when in 5th grade. The Rupars lived downtown in a nice home, and my mother, Darne,

*Mendel Hill at 5th Grade Birthday Party*

did housework for them. I remember enjoying the party especially since my mother was there. Mom was serving the spaghetti and generally making things work, just like she did at home on the hill. The social significance of that incident escaped me until years later. The second incident occurred when I was about 13 years old. I and my friends were playing a softball game that summer when Lew Smith and I almost got in a fight as I slid into 2nd base. As he and I danced (a typical fight in Elkland) without throwing a punch, I realized that all the other players were rooting for Smith and not one was rooting for me. Each of us, especially myself, grew up that day when our social structure made my "soon to be adult" teenage friends join the "club." From that day, we all remained friendly but were friends no more.

About the time of the softball game incident, I was diagnosed with a severe medical condition that required close observation from family. Normal teenage activities like sports and dating were out of the question. I did participate in school music activities, but my closest friend became the Elkland Library. Upon graduation, I attended Mansfield State College about 30 miles from Elkland. My brother, Manzo, Jr., was already enrolled there and could monitor my health status. Also, my mother, Darne, came to the college weekly to bring pies and cakes and to bring clean laundry. For the next two years, I had no recurring health problems, was a member of the eight-member Mansfield Madrigal Ensemble, sang a leading role in a college Christmas Operetta, and was a participant in a money making Rock and Roll Group, The Ivys, with my roommates. My two years at Mansfield were a wonderful experience. With health problems in the past and with the support of my parents who had pushed us to comfortably assimilate into the white world, I left college and sought the unknown challenges offered by the Army.

*Mendel practicing musing with four girl classmates*

*Mendel singing rock & roll with the Ivys in college*

After OCS and while being assigned to the 101st Airborne, I had an experience in Oxford, MS. My unit was sent to the University of Mississippi to quell the white radical instigators protesting James Meridith's entry into the school. Having never been to Mississippi (and never wanting to go there), I was shocked to watch a black man step off a sidewalk in Oxford so that a white person could pass. I grew to understand that that was a standard practice in Mississippi. Further, the Army brass decided that black soldiers could not participate in the riot formations. This was not acceptable to the black soldiers in my unit, and they protested. As the Colonel was conducting an all-black soldiers briefing explaining the decision, the soldiers became disrespectful. As the only black officer present, I interceded for the colonel, ordered/threatened the soldiers to show respect and halted the protest. If their protest (which I actually was proud of) had continued, they would have been sent to jail. One reason for that respect, I assume, is that as the assigned defense counsel for an obviously guilty black soldier who had wrecked a jeep while guarding the motor pool, my research found that he was charged with the wrong offense. The Board found him NOT GUILTY. I was a local hero among the black troops.

As my unit, the 502nd Infantry, was preparing for Vietnam service in the summer of 1964, my health condition returned after a seven year hiatus, and I was released from service. I was very disappointed to not serve a combat tour as my heroes had. I had been well trained with 36 parachute jumps and intensive jungle warfare exercises. I returned to college at American University in Washington, DC, to complete my bachelor's degree. The day after graduation on June 6, 1966, I was hired as a contract negotiator by NASA at the Goddard Space Flight Center. For the next 40 years, I became a seasoned bureaucrat helping NASA in its rush to the moon and as the first Business Manager for the developing International Space Station Project in 1987; working for the mayor's office in Washington, DC; managing a $300 million housing construction program for the state of California as a governor appointee in Los Angeles. After the housing job, I secured employment at the California Institute of Technology (Caltech) with the assistance of Edward Jasnow, my

NASA friend of 52 years. After retiring, I was employed at the Food and Drug Administration (FDA) assisting in the HIV research. At each stage of my professional life, I was required to overcome the barriers that all minorities and immigrants face.

### ◆ JOHN LEWIS

It is little wonder, based on John's close (and huge) family influences that he and his friends took that dangerous bus trip. Most of this background material is from John's book, *Walking with the Wind*, but I have offered a few highlights. John is a product of the union of great grandparents, Frank Carter and Bettie Baxter. Frank was born a slave, and he and his offspring remained in that area of Alabama for generations. Frank and his family eventually established a secure post-slavery compound named Carter's Quarters covering many acres. Frank and his children were tenant farmers graduating from leasing farms (Working on Half) to Standing Rent, where they owned the equipment and the mule but continued to lease. At holidays, there may be 400 relatives enjoying Frank's hospitality.

John's mother, Willie May, was one of 10 children fathered by John's grandfather Dink Carter. She married Eddie Lewis, who she had met at church when she was 18. John Robert Lewis was born the third child on February 21, 1940, with Bettie Carter, his great grandmother, acting as midwife. Youthful experiences of John's stand out to me. First, he had a determination to be educated. During planting season when he was obliged to support the family in cotton fields, John would hide under the house until the school bus arrived, and he would make a mad dash for it. That evening, he would receive a stern lecture from his father but never a whipping. Next day... the same. Second, his Uncle Otis Carter, a teacher and principal at a black school in the area, planned and took John on a summer trip to Buffalo, NY, to visit relatives. Experiencing blacks and whites living in harmony made the southern segregation practices unacceptable to John. Please note that at the same age as John, I would have the reverse geographical experience as I was taken on

*President Obama honoring Congressman John Lewis*

*Seco, Alabama Cotton Warehouse. John Lewis delivered grown cotton to the warehouse with his father.*

a family trip to visit great grandmother, Reed, in Memphis, TN. Third, brings me to the chickens, in his own words. "If there is a single point in my childhood that provided an early glimpse into my future, a first indication of what would come to shape my character and eventually guide me into the heart of the civil rights movement qualities I certainly could not name at the time, such as patience, compassion, nonviolence... it would be the year my parents gave me the responsibility of taking care of our family chickens." Enough to recount that the hen house seemed like a holy place to him, that they were so defenseless, that each morning he would take time to talk to them as he tended the straw in their nests, that he numbered each and every egg of the 60 hens during the three week hatch period. Fourth, John's first protest was at the Troy Library, as he could not obtain a membership card. His protest spirit escalated with Rosa Park's boycott and matured in 1958 at ABT nonviolent protests at the Nashville department stores and movie theaters. During this time, he joined up with James Lawson and Jim Zwerg.

After college, John became the national leader of the Student Nonviolent Coordinating Committee (SNCC). At the age of 23, John was selected to be a speaker at the famous 1963 March on Washington where Dr. King gave his "I Have a Dream" Speech, and John was attending meetings with the President and his staff. In 1965, John led 400 people to the Pettus Bridge in Selma, AL. While on the bridge, John and the marchers were viciously attacked by police and KKK members on horseback not only on the bridge but also throughout the town. Unsurprisingly, John was almost killed again (as in Montgomery) at what has come to be known as the "Bloody Sunday March." John went on to become a national leader as a member of Congress from Georgia since the 1980s. Surprisingly, with careers and goals so different, we came together for a short period as employees of the National Consumer Cooperative Bank in Washington, DC, in the early 80s. Researching subsequently, my wife and I embarked on a driving tour to the Troy, AL, area where John grew up and found the Seco warehouse and that Troy Library.

Life's realities touched both men's lives and should be mentioned. John's actions were part of the "Youth-Quake" energy of the southern youth in the

1960s. This was a rebuke of the conservative approaches (e.g., law suites, negotiations) used by the older generation of the NAACP, Thurgood Marshall and Churches. In the 1960s, four college students attending North Carolina A&T took it upon themselves to demand service at a whites-only Woolworths lunch counter. They were denied, but their actions seemed to inspire black college students throughout the south to engage. The new mantra was that personal safety was less important than securing your civil rights. One of those four brave souls went on to a successful career in the United States Air Force with the rank of General.

## REMEMBERING AND LAMENTING

The life challenges faced by the following individuals reflect the diversity of circumstances facing people during this era. The two names at the top of the list, Ernie Davis and Frankie Cox, were high school associates of mine who did not live beyond their 23rd and 29th birthdays, respectively. Both their early successes compounded by their early passing have tugged at my heart throughout my life as if they were one.

One summer day in 1955 or 1956, I joined a game being played on the old Neighborhood House basketball court. Soon I was challenged in a fight by a big, muscular player. Being new to the area, I prepared for a humiliating experience.

As the bully, Frankie Cox, moved in for the kill, a good Samaritan, equally big and muscular, moved between us and saved me. I later found out that both were budding sports stars at Elmira Free Academy. The good Samaritan was Ernie Davis. Thereafter, Ernie had my undying respect.

When Ernie and I would run into each other in later years, we would share some of the challenges we were facing in our world away from Elmira—his at Syracuse, mine in the Army.

Then came the devastating news in 1963 that Ernie had died of leukemia. There was no warning, no clue for his distant friends. The hero, the inspiration, was gone without a goodbye.

### ◆ ERNIE DAVIS

Ernie went on to a stellar college football career at Syracuse University and became the first black to win the Heisman Trophy, which was presented to him by President John F. Kennedy in New York City in 1961. In one conversation with him, Ernie discussed his experiences in Texas during the Cotton Bowl Game when Ernie's No. 1 ranked Syracuse Team played the No. 2 Texas Longhorns. He said the Texas players consistently called him a Nigger and punched him illegally after each tackle. Ernie responded with one of his

*Ernie Davis holding Heisman Trophy—1961*

*Ernie Davis meeting President Kennedy at Heisman ceremony*

better games, and Syracuse won to retain their No. 1 ranking and national championship. During that game, Ernie scored 16 of Syracuse's points, including a 87 yard record pass play. Typical of the times at this 1960 Cotton Bowl, Ernie was awarded the Most Valuable Player Award, but being black, he could only attend his ceremony and would have to depart immediately after. There were only three black players on the football team. Ernie refused to attend his Award Ceremony because he could only be present to accept the award. Not only did Ernie fail to attend, but his whole team of white players chose to not attend in honor of Ernie. After his death, Elmira honored him as follows:

Honors: (1) Ernie Davis Community Center; (2) Life-size bronze statue at Ernie Davis Middle School; (3) $12,000 Ernie Davis Annual Memorial Scholarship; (4) Ernie Davis Family Center with many community outreach programs.

Writing to the Saturday Evening Post, dated March 30, 1963, Ernie discussed his illness.

*I was never in pain, and I never felt sick. One July day (1962) I was practicing football with the College All-Stars going through*

54

*drills for a game against the Green Bay Packers. The next day I was in a hospital for many weeks without knowing why. I was afraid of what the doctors would say, so I didn't question them. Leukemia is a word that jumps out at you when I received my diagnosis in October 1962. The doctors told me it was in remission and there was no reason I couldn't play. Sometime along the line you have to come to an understanding with yourself. Either you fight or you die. For a time I was despondent. One day I got hold of myself. I decided I would face up to whatever I had and try to beat it. One day a stranger asked if I was Ernie Davis while I stood outside a theatre in Cleveland. Not wanting any fuss I told him no. The stranger said you are lucky. Davis has leukemia and won't live six months. There was nothing I could say. For all I knew the man could have been right.*

Ernie Davis passed away in 1963 of leukemia without playing a professional football game for the Cleveland Browns.


## ◆ FRANKIE COX

My first introduction to Frankie (the bully) at the age of 15 was very different from my last meeting with Frankie about 13 years later when I and he were both 28 years old. I had been discharged from military service four years earlier and was visiting friends in the town Elmira, NY, where I had initially met Frankie. Sitting at a local bar, I saw Frankie Cox waltz in resplendent in his Army Uniform, Lt. Bar on his shoulder, 101st Patch on his shoulder, Parachute wing on his chest, Ranger Insignia on his chest. Frankie had exceeded the military training I had achieved a few years earlier. We caught up on the past years, and then Frankie explained he was deploying to Vietnam in a few weeks. From growing up as a foster child to becoming a leader of men in wartime, Frankie had matured into a positive man in pursuit of life. We said a warm goodbye.

*Lt. Frankie Cox, baptized in Viet Nam—1968*

During combat operations in Vietnam while leading his Platoon, Frankie was killed when he stepped on a mine. It is important to note that, during the action, Frankie took the lead from Specialist Jerry Copeland and told him to manage the new troops from the rear. Copeland feels that his life was saved when Frankie took his place leading the platoon. Mr. Copeland made himself and his family available for a visit by me to their home outside of Tampa, FL, and he gave a firsthand account of the fighting that day. Mr. Copeland's daughter, Selena Ramsey, has made annual visits to the Vietnam Memorial Wall in Washington, DC, to pay homage to Frankie Cox. Also, in honor of Frankie, I have made contact with two of Frankie's children, Tony and Tammy. Frankie Cox received the Bronze Star for his heroic action. The following words were written by Celena Ramsey, daughter of Jerry Copeland, about Frankie Cox.

> *All of my life I have heard your story, but until only recently did I hear your name. We spent years and hit many dead ends trying to find out the name of the officer who was so seriously wounded walking point for my father and whether or not he (you) were*

*still alive. You didn't have to walk point that day, you were an officer. But you never belittled your E.M. My dad was carrying the starlight scope and should not have been walking point either. So you took over for him. They said you died instantly but you didn't. You lost 3 limbs and the 4th was barely hanging on, but you were still alive, <u>awake and yelling out orders</u>, looking out for your men, when Daddy picked you up and put you on the chopper. That's almost unimaginable. When the door gunner came back around, he said you were dead, so my father always thought you had to be.*

*In our quest to find you, everyone who remembered you thought the world of you too. I used to picture myself talking to you, imagining what I would say, what you would say, if we could somehow find you and you were alive. I am so glad we finally found you, I know it meant a lot to my dad but man, how we all wish we could've found you alive. We've looked for your family (to no avail). My father would like to tell them what a wonderful person he knew you to be, but I know they know.*

## STORIES AND LESSONS

Webster's Dictionary defines courage as a mental or moral strength to venture, persevere and withstand danger, fear or difficulty. The following personal stories detect a host of dramatic examples of courage displayed by ordinary citizens. The stories further reflect other personal important attributes like self-confidence, determination, grit, family support, and educational achievement. It is hoped that the reader can reflect on the unique strengths depicted and apply them to their own set of circumstances.

### ◆ JAMES F. BERRY

James is a man in his middle 80s who obtained a BS degree in Electrical Engineering from the University of Southern California after seven years of night school and part time study. He earned his MSEE under a Hughes Aircraft Company Masters Fellowship and later in his career utilized this education and experience to become a corporate leader in the National Defense Industry. Jesse is also an inventor, designer of passive Sonar Systems, and author of numerous technical articles appearing in multiple technology journals while also a family man with four highly educated and distinguished children who hold multiple undergraduate, graduate, and law degrees.

Born in Asheville, NC, he moved with his parents to Cleveland, OH, while in elementary school. His early displayed mathematical interests and skills allowed him to set obtaining an electrical engineering degree as a primary goal.

Jesse spent two years serving in the U.S. Army which, laughingly continually misplaced him in job assignments (posted to an Army Hospital Emergency Room after completing Construction Engineer Surveying training). Upon Discharge, Jesse returned to Cleveland and began his pursuit of a career in engineering. Attending a job fair at a Cleveland Employment Office, Jesse met and impressed a North American Aviation corporate recruiter. Since Jesse did not yet have a BS degree, the recruiter could not hire hm in Cleveland and offered to find him a technical position when and if Jesse lived in the Los Angeles, CA, area.

Albeit his professional attainments in subsequent years, there were two early personal barriers that Jesse had to face and overcome First, he had to get to California, and second, he had to obtain an engineering degree. Six months after the employment office interview, Jesse, without a job, packed his wife and belongings into the family car and, with the aid of "The Green Book," drove to Los Angeles. Upon arrival, he contacted the recruiter who found him a position in the research laboratory at North American Aviation. Having arrived in Los Angeles and found employment, Jesse's next goal was to become a graduate engineer. He enrolled in the Electrical Engineering program at the University of Southern California. During the enrollment process, Jesse and the one other black student were advised that they lacked the intelligence required to successfully pursue a degree in Electrical Engineering. Barrier II fell when, despite the advice, he and the other black student completed all of USC's requirements and graduated with BSEE degrees.

## CAREER PROGRESSION

| | | |
|---|---|---|
| 1959 - 1971 | North American Aviation | Lab Technician |
| 1962 - 1966 | Interstate Electronics | Jr. Engineer |
| 1966 - 1971 | Hughes Aircraft Company | Electronics Engineer |
| 1972 - 1973 | Honeywell Corporation | Principal Engineer |
| 1974 - 1978 | Hughes Aircraft Company | Group Supervisor |
| 1978 - 1980 | General Dynamics Corp. | Program Manger |
| 1980 - 1993 | Vitro Corporation | Department Head |
| | | Director Technology Div. |
| | | Principal Associate |
| 1994 - 2007 | JB Enterprises | Founder/Owner |

◆ OTIS WRIGHT

Otis is a man in his mid-80s of moderate wealth who has (1) been successful in both business and academia, (2) been a family man with three college educated children, (3) maintained a happy marriage with his wife Gertherine, and (4) has a deep love for his country that he calls the land of opportunity. Otis was born of a single mother in rural Arkansas in the 1930s. Otis' mother was killed when he was six months old, and he was raised by a loving grandmother who preached into his young ears that he must get an education. At the age of 12, with no local schools available to a black beyond 7th grade, Otis joined a distant relative in Ogden, UT, and obtained work.

At the age of 17, Otis returned to Arkansas and negotiated an entry into 10th grade. He obtained his high school diploma at 20 and sought acceptance into a black university located in Pine Bluff, AR. He was accepted into a work-study program and completed two years. At that point, Otis volunteered for the U.S. Army during the Korean War, served two years part of which was in Korea, and returned to the university with the assistance of the GI Bill. Upon graduation, Otis secured his wife Gertherine (who had withheld marriage until he had a college degree) and moved to Los Angeles, CA. Both Otis and Gertherine had teaching careers, started business careers, and more importantly, maintained a strong supportive family structure which produced college graduations for each of their three offspring. I have known Otis for over 30 years, and he is one of my life heroes.

### ◆ TUSKEGEE AIRMEN

The Tuskegee Airmen Pilot Training Program was initiated in 1941 at Tuskegee Institute in Alabama. It took strong lobbying by Black Americans to convince the government that blacks could operate airplanes. One day, Eleanor Roosevelt visited the training program and wanted to be taken up in flight with one of the black pilots. Upon completion of the flight, she was personally aware that black pilots could fly.

I interviewed Lt. Col. Hiram E. Mann one of the originally trained pilots in his Florida home. He told stories of his training and particularly his combat missions over Germany and Eastern Europe from his base in Italy. Hiram was born in the south, but grew up in Cleveland, Ohio. After high school, he began college in Arkansas. He then qualified for training at Tuskegee. I asked Hiram what motivated him to want to fight in a war for the United States when he lived in such a segregated society.

He said, "I wanted to kill Germans, and the social issues can be addressed later."

I did not have an opportunity to interview Captain Lawrence E. Dickson, 24, one of 27 Tuskegee Airmen listed as missing when his P-51 Mustang went down over Italy on December 23, 1944. Captain Dickson was one of over 900 black pilots trained at the segregated Army Air Field in Alabama and was one of more than 400 who served in combat in North Africa and

Italy. He took off from his base at Ramitelli in southern Italy with two other comrades in their P-51 Ds escorting a reconnaissance plane to Prague, Czechoslovakia. Captain Dickson was on his 68th mission when he would have been eligible for R&R back home after his 70th. His wingman, 2nd Lt. Robert L. Martin, recounted that white pilots were eligible for R&R after only 50 missions. Captain Dickson was survived by his wife Phyllis Dickson and his daughter Marla L. Andrews.

### ◆ JAMES LAWSON

Mr. Lawson was born in Pennsylvania in 1928 and grew up in Ohio. It is my opinion that he is one of the most influential activists of the modern civil rights era. First, while a freshman at Baldwin Wallace College in Berea, OH, he became an advocate for nonviolent resistance to racism. So committed, he became a conscientious objector and refused to report for the draft, which earned him 14 months in prison.

After release, he went to India to study the Gandhi principles of nonviolence resistance. Upon his return, he entered the Graduate School of Theology at Oberlin College and, while there, was introduced to Martin Luther King, Jr., who had participated in the Montgomery Bus Boycott. King and Lawson maintained a good collaborative friendship (1) as King advised Lawson to move south and promote nonviolence in the black community and (2) as Lawson asked King to come to Memphis, TN, to support the garbage strike. There, King gave his "Mountaintop" speech and was assassinated on the very next day.

When Lawson, following King's advice, moved south, he settled in Nashville, where he trained the future civil rights leaders in the tactics of nonviolence which they successfully applied. Some of the names are John Lewis, Diane Nash, James Bevel, Marion Barry. His students participated in the Freedom Rides, the 1963 March on Washington, The Mississippi Summer Project, and the Anti-Vietnam War Movement in the late 60s.

### ◆ MRS. RECY TAYLOR

Mrs. Recy Taylor was walking home with two friends from a late night church service in Abbeville, AL, on September 3, 1944. A car filled with white youth approached the group and abducted Mrs. Taylor. Each of the young men raped her and left her on a deserted road with instructions that they would kill her if she told. Recy and her family reported the rape to the town authorities; a confession was obtained but two grand juries failed to return an indictment. Ironically, an investigator was assigned by the local branch of the NAACP in Montgomery to gather the facts from Mrs. Taylor. The investigator sent was Mrs. Rosa Parks. Mrs. Parks went to Abbeville but was ordered out of town by the local Sheriff. Mrs. Taylor, threatened that she would be killed, continued to pursue her lawsuit as the first black woman to do so. There is not a person in the world who I respect more than Mrs. Recy Taylor.

### ◆ MRS. FANNIE LOU HAMER

A discussion on women in the civil rights movement cannot be concluded without honoring Mrs. Fannie Lou Hamer, who resides in the Mississippi Delta town of Greenwood. On June 9, 1963, Mrs. Hamer and a group of SNCC female volunteers were arrested in Winona, MS. Each woman was beaten and sexually abused by the custody police. They first assaulted a 16-year-old by forcing her to strip as they beat her. As they beat a second woman with black jacks, they kept ordering her to say "Yes, Sir, Nigger." Mrs. Hamer was beaten by the police and also by two black inmates who were forced to beat her. Mrs. Hamer did give testimony at the Democratic National Convention in 1964 and to congressional investigators.

### ◆ JO ANN ROBINSON

Women like Jo Ann Robinson (the leader) and the maids and cooks who kept walking for 381 days are the ones who deserve the credit for the success of the Montgomery Bus Boycott. Compromise negotiations were conducted by the black leaders through the whole boycott period, but the working women's resolve dictated the final result.

The onus is on each of us Black Americans to be a part of the efforts to develop a culture blanket that will make each competitive. There must be a complete devotion to family, to love and support each other, to ensure education opportunities for each child and to emphasize financial strength training. One first step could be the development of political strength via voting. To be a member off the Black American culture, your first duty is to vote at every opportunity. A model to be followed would be what the 24-year-old Reverend King imposed on his new congregation. In order to be a member of his church, you had to vote. Other examples to be replicated regarding education are the uniquely successful schools in Newark and Chicago that produce black youth who are high achievers and who are supportive of each other.

Our culture must be able to accomplish two seemingly opposite initiatives successfully. While focusing on developing a strong black cultural identity, we must be conscious of and supportive of a final push towards ASSIMILATION and BICULTURALISM for all of us.

## ◆ DR. WYATT TEE WALKER - MINISTER

Of the many accomplished activists I was fortunate enough to interview, Dr. Walker is the one that left me with an unforgettable impression of warmth and wisdom. Dr. Walker was born in Brockton, MA, to parents who graduated from the first Virginia Union College class in 1899. After high school in 1946, he attended Virginia Union and graduated in 1950 with degrees in Physics and Chemistry. In that same year, he married his classmate Theresa Ann Walker, and they raised four children. Dr. Walker obtained his Masters in Divinity in 1953.

Dr Walker's life had many highlights:

- Ordained in 1952
- Ministered Gillfield Baptist Church (seven years), Petersburg, VA
- Joined Martin Luther King, Jr. at the Southern Christian Leadership Conference (SCLC) for four years as chief strategist experiencing jailings with Dr. King
- Ministered for 37 years as Pastor at Harlem's Canaan Baptist Church of Christ in New York City, and Ministered at Abyssinian Baptist Church replacing Congressman and Minister Adam Clayton Powell

I interviewed Dr. Walker with his wife Theresa and three children in attendance. The warmth and concern expressed by the whole family was amazing. The Dr. and his wife told many stories of their experiences in the south working with the SCLC. Theresa, by the way, experienced many dangerous situations on her own while supporting her husband and protecting her four children.

Before concluding the interview, I asked Dr. Walker, "What was the major accomplishment of the black church for black people?"

Dr. Walker responded with one word, "HOPE!"

# 7

# BLACK AND WHITE:
## THE TANGO

The relationship between blacks and the white society is unique and much more dynamic than that of the other immigrant ethnics that have settled the United States. This unique relationship started with the beginning of our nation. In 1787, the Continental Congress included the Three-Fifths Compromise into the Constitution in Article 1, Section 2, Paragraph 3. In essence, for Representation and Direct Taxes, slaves and indentured servants as three fifths of a person. Not directly acknowledging slavery, the Constitution, spells out "three-fifths of all other persons," excluding Indian, not taxed. From our beginning, blacks have been an integral part of our voting and taxation base, been an integral part of our economic progress, and been a willing collaborator/associate in all national actions, including wars.

It is the position here that the United States has always been a nation of color (black and white), not a white nation. It is also the position here that the courage and selflessness of the modern civil rights era activists, while imposing a death knoll on the dual fantasy of white privilege/control, also opened the door for our confirmed bicultural society of blacks, whites, Asians, Indians, and Hispanics. We now face immigration and white nationalist issues here and around the world, especially in Western Europe. The question is: What is the best prescription to solve these problems? I think the answer resides in an objective look at our slow, exhausting progress.

The relationship between the blacks and whites clarifies if one views it as a collaborative dependence. The metaphorical similarity between a slave and master is based on their mutual dependence as in a tango dance. The tango is a partner dance, a mating dance commanded by the male lead; yet the male lead must be constantly aware of his mate's abilities and rhythms. While exerting control through rape and lynching, the dominate whites must supply the basic needs of their chattel in order to achieve their wealth and security. This dance, however, also incorporates an expected counter rhythms that bring closeness and intimacy.

The Tuskegee fighter pilots in World War II provided perfect protection for the white crews of the vulnerable bombers flying missions over enemy territory. While initially resistant to black pilots being assigned to provide them protection, their prejudice turned into acceptance and admiration when their bomber losses ceased when black pilots accompanied them. White Christians went south after the Civil War to start over 40 colleges for the education of former slaves; abolitionist whites established and assisted in the Underground Railroad System that helped fleeing slaves. The white businesses in the north went through great efforts to recruit black laborers from the south for their factories during the Great Migration to the north.

*Tuskegee Airmen Monument, Walterboro, SC*

*Lt. Hill and 101st Airborne buddies—Officers Club party*

The United States has developed a template for a successful development of a multi-ethnic, integrated social platform. It was developed over a period of 400 years of trial and error, compromises, and the mixing of the best and worst of our human nature. The following personal stories provide a sense of the pathos, the drama, and the related humanity, both good and bad, of our society.

## THE HARMONY OF TEAM WORK - JOHN LEWIS

I had gained an interview with the now Congressman John Lewis on April 15, 2015, to gain firsthand information on his involvement in the Civil Rights struggle of the 1960s. He did provide a good perspective on his past experiences. As I was departing his office, John's last words of advice were, "Don't forget the help that Jews provided."

## A TRIPLE TANGO - CHARLES EVERS' TALK

There is a simple story told to me by Charles Evers, older brother of the assassinated Medgar Evers, about his experience growing up in Decatur, MS. Charles told me that his father, Jim Evers, was the only man he knew of in Mississippi who refused to step off the sidewalk when a white person approached. I suppose that Jim's example led to the youths' strong behavior as adults.

His second story is about a white man who had become angry with him. Charles and Medgar had to walk eight or nine miles to school each day from Decatur. To make life easier for himself, Charles worked for Ms. Payne in her restaurant in Newton where he could attend the Newton Negro School. He lived in the attic above the store for several years and completed through the 10th grade in Newton. One day, a mean white customer confronted Charles and became very threatening and used the "nigger" phrase aggressively. Ms. Payne protected Charles, ordering the man out of the restaurant with instructions never to return.

A third point made by Charles refers to Medgar's assassin, Beckwith. Charles stated that Medgar was such a sweet man that, if Beckwith had ever spoken to Medgar, he would not have shot him. That statement, to me, reflects on the unique relationship that existed between blacks and whites in the south.

## A JOURNEY OF LOVE ~ JIM ZWERG'S EXPERIENCE

*Jim Zwerg and wife Carrie—2016*
*Lunch in Gallop, NM with Mendel and Helen*

The reader was first introduced to Jim in the PROLOGUE when he rode the bus with John Lewis in the spring of 1961.

As my wife Helen and I were concluding our lunch interview with Jim Zwerg and his wife Carrie in Gallup, NM, on August 12, 2017, Jim repeatedly lamented the fact that he had not continued the interstate bus trip that had resumed while he was hospitalized with the brutal beatings he had received at the Montgomery Bus Station weeks before. Of the riders who had been attacked, Jim received the worst of the beatings and the only long-term hospital stay. Yet, even 50 years later, he carries a guilt for not being able to support them as they moved into harm's way again.

A year and a half before our first meeting at the interview, Jim responded on January 1, 2016, to some questions I had forwarded. His response is included here in his own words:

*Hi Mendel*

*There were three things that influenced me when I was younger.*

*My parents primarily. They introduced me to classical music and literature, poetry, respect for others, organization of belonging and thoughts, maintenance of toys, bicycles, tools, etc. They encouraged my brother and me to always do our best to any endeavor. My mother was constantly reminding us that we were the sons of a professional man (a dentist) and that we should never say or do anything to tarnish his good name.*

*Both parents led by example. I can't recall ever hearing a prejudicial remark about other faiths, nationalities, etc. They were both active in various service organizations and volunteered their time supporting our activities.*

*Another major influence during my formative years was the Boy Scouts of America. I went through all the levels of Cub Scouts, achieved the rank of Eagle Scout and in early high school joined the explorer Scouting program. I took to heart the scout Oath, Motto, and Laws.*

*"On my honor, I promise to do my duty to God and my country, to obey the Scout Laws, to help other people at all times to keep myself physically strong, mentally awake and morally straight."*

*"Be prepared."*

*"A Scout is trustworthy, loyal, helpful, courteous, kind, obedient, cheerful, thrifty, brave, clean and reverent."*

*"Do a good turn daily."*

*These were more than words to me. I believed them and did my best to put them into practice in my everyday life. Scouting remained a major influence until my later years in high school when I discovered girls.*

Ours was a church going family. I had attended Sunday school regularly, became an acolyte, sung in youth and adult choirs, and joined the rest of the family in occasionally serving as ushers or greeters. Then, the end of my junior year, I was elected president of the high school youth group. about that time our Senior Minister left for another church. The Assistant/Youth Minister asked if the Youth Group would lead a service once a month. We agreed. I was chosen to give the sermon. It was very well received and many commented that I would make a good minister. Our Youth Minister, Dick Schroeder, seemed to agree. He took me "under his wing" and introduced me to various aspects of the ministry. He took me on home and hospital visits. He was a warm caring pastor with the gift of sensing what to say or do in the way of comfort or encouragement. He stressed the importance of putting one's faith into action. I began to consider the possibility of my becoming a minister. I knew I wanted to work with people and to make a difference but wasn't certain how that would be manifested in my life.

*Why did I subject myself to the risks? That's an easy question to answer. I had seen something in John Lewis and the other students who were members of the Nashville Movement. It was the power of love that was manifest in nonviolent direct action. As I attended the workshops on nonviolence, I would reread the Scripture passages that were cited. I wrestled with my faith and lack of putting it into practice. And I prayed. Then one day, I realized that the Christian Gospels told the story of the most amazing proponent of nonviolence who ever lived. Jesus. He turned the other cheek. He loved and forgave his enemies. He endured innocent suffering. Nonviolence direct action was what Jesus had used. I committed myself to do likewise and embraced nonviolence as my way of life. I became an active participant in Sit-ins and Stand-ins. I was selected to become a member of the Central Committee, the more experienced and proven student leaders who planned the demonstrations and help lead the workshops. I was never so spiritually alive! My reading of Scripture became more meaningful. Prayer provided comfort and courage. I was never so sure that I was following God's will. When we decided to continue the Freedom Ride I volunteered to go. I also knew there was a very real possibility that I would be killed, but I also knew my place was to be on the bus.*

*Hope this will provide some insight,*

*Jim*

## TWO DIFFERENT RESULTS - MENDEL HILL

### ◆ 1965 – MENDEL'S TRAFFIC STOP

It was a hot summer evening around 10 PM in Washington DC, as I drove the dark streets trying to find a pizza shop that my wife had recommended. I was tired after a full day of classes at American University plus four hours of work at the liquor store where I was employed part time. After completing five years of military service, I had moved to Washington to obtain my bachelor's degree.

After circling several blocks and not finding my pizza target, I noticed a police car with lights blazing on my tail. I became very apprehensive because I was aware of several driving requirements (e.g., expired driver's license, expired state tags) that I had temporally ignored due to my limited funds. I was anticipating fines that my limited student budget could not afford.

As I was searching for the required document, I nervously dropped the contents of my wallet on the ground. The two white officers assisted in picking up the papers and suddenly became friendlier towards me. The conversation went like this:

"You were in the 101st Airborne Division?"

"Yes I was!"

"You were an Officer?"

"Yes, a 1st Lt!"

"You attend American U?"

"Yes I do!"

"You have a busted tail light, you have an expired Kentucky driver's license, you have out-of-state tags, and you are driving the wrong direction on this one-way street!"

The two officers stepped away momentarily to hold a discussion. When they returned, they handed me a warning ticket and said they would come by my residence in a month to ensure that my violations had been corrected. I thanked them and drove my 12-year-old car straight home. No pizza, but I had received an amazing, unexpected reprieve.

## ◆ 2016 – PHILANDO'S TRAFFIC STOP

It was late afternoon in Falcon Heights, MI. Philando was driving with his girlfriend Diamond Reynolds in the passenger seat and their four (4) year old daughter tucked in the back seat. Philando worked in an elementary school cafeteria. Police Officer Geronimo Yanez noticed a faulty break light and pulled Philando over. As he produced his documentation, he also advised the officer that he had a permit to carry a firearm. As Philando reached in his pocket the officer fired five bullets into his body killing him instantly. The officer was found not guilty of manslaughter.

The experiences of myself and Philando, albeit 50 years apart, is this book's opening door to a peak at our society of tomorrow. We were both wearing our black skin. I had been reminded over time that I was black and intellectually inferior. I recall my white college teacher accused me of cheating because I carried an "A" in English Philology. My Gunnery instructor in OCS accused me of cheating when I got a perfect score on a test. My Army unit was sent to Oxford, MS, to quell the white riots at the University of Mississippi intent on preventing the enrollment of James Meredith. The Army brass decided that black soldiers would not participate in the riot formations on the campus, and we did not. I am sure that Philando had experienced the same reminders on a regular basis.

Only upon reading the tragic story of Philando did my memory go back to my similar experience 50 years ago. Why was Philando murdered while I was given a generous reprieve? Would you, the reader, develop your own personal answer before reading on?

My conclusion is (1) I was black when I was stopped, and (2) I was admired (white) when the policemen saw my credentials. Philando was equally black when stopped. When he was questioned without credentials, he was observed a dangerous black. Based on the above, it is obvious why we were perceived so differently. That answer dictates a solution. The solution is that our black culture must guarantee that everyone of us meet a standard that provides a secure certainty. It was not Philando's fault that he was murdered. It is our weak cultural trait that did not embrace him with our collective energy. Did he have parents like mine who treated my brother and me like princes? Did he have strong family support that pushed for education? I now realize that those two police officers, on their own, elevated me to the "white" cultural status. Sadly, Philando paid the price for being observed as dangerous both culturally and physically.

## When the Music Stopped - Mickey and Rita Schwerner

In 1964, two years after my experience in Mississippi, an idealistic 24-year-old Jewish man from New York volunteered for and was hired to be a CORE field worker in Mississippi for the purpose of increasing black voting. His name was Michael "Mickey" Schwerner, and he and his wife Rita were assigned to the eastern Mississippi city of Meridian. Because of Mickey's work with the black community, Mickey was targeted by the Mississippi Ku Klux Klan for elimination. In June, Mickey and two associates, Andrew Goodman and James Chaney, were murdered by Klan members. Based on my previous experience in Mississippi, the CORE management team in Jackson did not assess the certain danger Mickey, his wife, and his associates were placed in.

Mickey graduated from Cornell University and attended Columbia University seeking a graduate degree in the School of Social Work. Even though Mickey received hate mail and threatening phone calls, he believed that Mississippi was the decisive battleground for overcoming white supremacy. In this dangerous job, Mickey received $9.80 per week.

I have recently had the pleasure of communicating with Mickey's widow Rita. Rita has established a successful legal practice since her tragic circumstances in Mississippi. I will include the substance of a letter in response to my correspondence. I value her opinion and thoughts because she is an historic figure and because she and Mickey had the courage and determination to provide assistance to the less fortunate notwithstanding the cost.

*June 24, 2015*
*Mr. Hill:*

*By now you have likely moved on with the interviews of John Lewis and others and perhaps have some more sense the answer to the question you pose. I honestly don't that I can answer the "why," because when I try, it seems simplistic. A Movement is many people with almost as many life experiences. While mine was a working class family, I certainly was the beneficiary of white privilege, although it took many years to understand that.*

*When I look at where we are as a country now, it is hard to feel very optimistic. Yes, for some people possibilities have opened up. But many have been left behind. While the "badges and indi-*

cia" of slavery and racism are in the news this week, and the Confederate flag may finally be retired, I'm not at all sure that the
deeper issues of systemic racism will be confronted. In fact there
is a very strong push against such acknowledgment.

I'm certainly not saying anything which you don't already
know. But I did want to return your photos and let you know I
hadn't forgotten your very personal letter.

My best,
Rita

The civil rights movement was supported by many in the Jewish community.
Jewish students worked with many of the black organizations including
CORE, SCLC, and SNCC as full-time organizers and summer volunteers
during the 1964 Mississippi Freedom Summer project seeking increases in
black voting rights.

The comments of both Jim and Rita bring to life the traumatic and
deadly experiences suffered by determined black and white youth in that
phase of the civil rights movement. How many of us reading these accounts
would have taken these challenges. Mickey and his associates paid with their
lives, and I am sure they willingly accept the risks. I offer the following words
to both, Jim and Rita.

"Because of the purposeful courage and humanity in your hearts,
our society is moving slowly, haltingly to a better place. Do not
despair! Celebration is in order!"

*Mrs. Rita Schweren Bender—age 23—1964*
*Husband Mickey murdered by KKK*

*Mrs. Rita Schweren Bender—age 78*
*Lawyer, activist—2018*

*Friends Mendel Hill and Edward Jasnow delivering Rotary Grant checks to teachers*

# 8

# ECONOMICS:

## THE ELEPHANT IN THE ROOM

This chapter will provide the reader with the dominating essence of our economic system, will identify the systemic barriers imposed on the average citizens, and will provide an analysis of how and why the economic system established centuries ago remains in effect even today. Two points need to be made. First, all economic decisions, with few exceptions, made in this country are made to enhance and sustain the perpetual dominance of the oligarchy, the business community and the state. Second, the tool employed to sustain this dominance is the skillful application of the art of hypocrisy.

## THE FOUR ECONOMIC PILLARS

While there are many ways to describe our economic order, I see it simply as the four cooperating pillars that provide an easy assessment. The Oligarchy (very rich 1 percent), the Business Community and the State (Federal and State Government). These three pillars purposely have a supportive foundation of free (slavery) or cheap (immigrant) labor that ensures their profitability and continuity. The fourth pillar, hypocrisy, justifies or provides cover for the three other elements of the hierarchical (make believe) order. Without the African Slave Trade, the western nations' internal economies would not have flourished and the United States' agricultural growth could not have been sustained.

## FREE AND CHEAP LABOR

In the 13th Century, Albert Mangus, a Dominican Bishop, probably put economic theory into western thought. He proposed that the cost of production must be considered when determining value. Other writers like Gerald Adonis, a French Monk, added weight to thoughts on labor and wages. It does seem, however, that Edgar Furniss in his classic work, "The Positions of the Laborer in a System of Nationalism," matured these philosophies. He generally argued that laborers should be kept "at the margins of subsistence." He further argued that the oligarchy (moneyed people) and the business class must ensure that labor wages remain low. He called it the "Utility of Poverty" since high wages would lead the poor to excesses. This terrible philosophy has been bought into and implemented by these Western Nations and the United States through today.

I maintain that Furniss' warnings have been successfully applied in two distinct but related stages. I call the first stage the Free Labor (slavery) Stage that lasted 400 or 500 years. Due to advances in ship building and navigation improvements, the western nations could sail to Africa and Asia to acquire the slave (free) labor needed for their economic growths. From around 1500 to the middle of the 19th century, free labor was the engine that supported and sustained the economic growth of the west. Free labor was not only slave labor but also indentured servants who actually were in use prior to slaves in many instances. The wealth accruing to the nations based on free labor was tremendous. It is estimated that 300,000 sailors were employed in the slave trade. The shipbuilding industry sustained local economics like England's Bristol and Liverpool. Prior to the Civil War, eight of the 10 million-aires in the U.S. were southern plantation owners. Without free labor, the western European nations and particularly the United States would not have the dominant economic roles they hold today.

With the end of slavery (free labor) in the United States in 1865, the second stage of controlling the cost of labor began with the cheap labor policies. These government sanctioned policies, encouraged and supported by the oligarchy and business community, clearly sustained the economic engine that supported them. I have identified two principle elements that are ingenious substitutes for free labor, and I am sure these two are just the tip of the iceberg. The first substitute combined (1) the southern Sharecropping practice where former slaves entered into a business relationship with white land owners and (2) the north's immigration policies that brought low skilled cheap laborers who were also financially exploited. This practice even extended to the rest of the Americas. After slavery was abolished in Brazil, Brazil extended immigration to thousands of Japanese citizens with the same exploitive practices employed against the new workers as were employed in the United States.

The second substitute is the Minimum Wage laws and practices that impact the lives of low skilled workers today. On the surface, they identify an hourly rate (e.g., $7.50 or $12.50) that must be paid at a minimum. In actual practice, however, these identified minimums operate as a maximum rate. First, the rates established are so low that a person working a 40-hour week will remain in poverty. Second, increases in the poverty sustaining rates are resisted by the oligarchy, business, and government at every turn. The centuries old dictum of Edgar Furniss, that the oligarchy and business classes "ensure" that labor wages remain low has been sustained in this modern era. His "Utility of Poverty" is the backbone of our economic system.

# THE INSIDIOUS WEAPON · HYPOCRISY

## INSIDIOUS; (1) AWAITING A CHANCE TO ENTRAP, (2) HARMFUL BUT ENTICING AND (3) TREACHEROUS

The second subject of the two is the issue of Hypocrisy that the super rich use to stay in political power. As part of the 2016 presidential election, the Republican candidate, a member of the oligarchy and business class, gained the winning votes primarily from middle class and lower class white citizens. He preached a message that addressed their fears, yet had no intention to help them on health or jobs. The fearful message addressed immigrants, who were Mexican "rapists," "bad hombres," and terrorist Muslims. The most obvious hypocrisy, however, is stating that the immigrants will take the poor white man's job.

This point is addressed in Aimé Césaire's Discourse on Colonialism". Aimé was a Frenchman born in Martinique, received his college education in Paris and became a noted writer.

> The facts that the so-called European civilization Western civilization as it has been shaped by two centuries of bourgeois rule, is incapable of solving the two major problems to which its existence has given rise. The problem of the proletariat and the colonial problems, that Europe is unable to justify itself either before the bar of "reason" or before the bar of "conscience" , and that, increasingly, it takes refuge in a hypocrisy which is all the more odious because it is less and less likely to deceive.

The following is an actual list of typical hypocrisy statements typically used by our Presidents down to the average citizens.

### ECONOMIC

- Immigrants will compete for your job.
- Immigrants go on welfare.
- We will bring back jobs lost to other countries.

## SOCIAL

- Immigrants bring their bad culture.
- Civil Rights activists are communists.
- Muslims are terrorists.
- Mexicans are rapists.
- Immigration will destroy our white culture.

# 9

# THE NEW SOCIETY

The INTRODUCTION pointed us towards our unique and diverse cultural platform that successfully developed our country. It also pointed out that the arrival of numerous immigrant groups and their subsequent assimilation (albeit delayed repeatedly by barriers) into the dominant English culture has been a political objective since our founding.

There are certain patterns in our history that demand our attention and understanding if citizens are to improve our status in society, if we are to overcome the societal barriers created to maintain the status quo rules not in our favor. Some, but not all, of these patterns are listed below.

- Social stratification has been part of human social patterns for thousands of years in human existence. One may think it is unfair that oligarchs garner an inappropriate amount of our economic resources, but that result is a result of our human instincts. Fairness need not apply for consideration.

- There will always be at least three layers in all of the various societies created by humans, and that principle is embedded in our United States society. The working poor will always be assigned to the exploited bottom layer be they black or white.

- Strong cultural traits will always be the perfect antidote to barriers designed to impede the assimilation of immigrant groups.

- Basic human instincts (e.g., fear, self-protection, love) will always be at play in our daily social discourse. Otherwise, how do we explain slavery, public lynchings, NAZI exterminations? These acts are a natural part of human behavior.

- Individuals or groups must always be prepared to pivot away from old standards, previously thought to be adequate and comfortable when societal circumstances change and dictate change. The pivot of the Irish in the 1840s away from an anti-slavery position is a prime example. The pivot of the upper class Jews in the 1890s to embrace the less educated immigrant eastern European Jews is a prime example. The pivot of our national government (supported by business and political entities) away from slavery while replacing it with share cropping is a prime example. It can be predicted that these same entities will pivot towards the coming bicultural society as evidenced by growth of TV commercials depicting bicultural subjects. At least 40 to 50 percent of commercials include people of color. Fifty years ago, few commercials included people of color.

- If you think that the members of the Four Pillars (Government, Business, Oligarchy) will cease and desist from imposing their most effective control asset HYPOCRISY, you are sadly mistaken. It has been used effectively in the past (blacks are not human - Supreme Court's Justice Tanney; Mexicans are rapists - President Trump) and will be used in our tomorrows. Citizens must be able to separate "the wheat from the shaft," unless it satisfies your existing human prejudices and fears.

- The dominant culture will constantly develop ASSIGNMENTS for minorities or immigrants that are designed to keep them in the "less than equal" status in perpetuity. Some examples are the

160-year support for HBCUs and minority business programs. When the recipient accepts these devious amenities, they confirm their own acceptance of the "less than equal" status of said assignment.

The fast moving changes to our society dictated by the browning of America are having a marked impact on two specific immigrant groups. The first group, not surprisingly, is the Black Americans who have not assimilated and who lack the necessary cultural strengths, on their own, to reap the rewards of America. The second group, surprisingly, is the white working class members who have discarded their immigrant energies for the benefits accruing from the white privileges bestowed. In the future, privileges will only be reserved for all peoples (black, white, brown) who meet the new criteria (educated, financially secure, and amalgamated socially).

# 10

# ADMONITION TO
# BLACK AMERICANS

The black culture in America is a work in progress. That progress needs to continue so that it will eventually exhibit the strength combinations that have sustained the other arriving immigrant groups. This is not to imply that the cultural development in the black community has been a failure. In fact, it has been a success occurring over four centuries. As the Irish Catholics or Japanese arrived on day one with fully formed cultures, blacks had to focus on individual survival day one. While the Jews, for instance, could apply their existing culture strengths to overcome the imposed barriers and to start the assimilation process, blacks would be required to wait 250 years (until Emancipation) before we could start to develop the strength elements (e.g., family, collectivism) needed in our culture. So for the past 150 years, a black culture has been developing but progressing slowly against the stiff winds of barriers like exploitation, Jim Crow, discrimination, and bad cultural weaknesses. In these past 150 years, the black people of our country have been equal participants in the development of our country just as any other citizen or ethnic group from wars to building our cities to building our infrastructures. We can get a pass on cultural development, but now we need to pivot to our culture as a priority.

This is my assessment of our growth towards a strong Black American culture as of today.

## COLLECTIVISM

I have found little or no evidence that the existing black culture places great emphasis on working together for the common good or that the interests of the individual are, or at times can be, subordinate to the group. The life examples provided by the Japanese Bessho family must be absorbed and incorporated into our culture patterns if we are going to become culturally strong.

## FAMILY

In general, the black family is not in a positive circumstance particularly in the lower economic strata. Many children are born into fatherless homes to an alarming degree. I grew up with my father at home each day setting an example in close coordination with my mother. Otis Wright and his wife Gertherine worked as a team on a daily basis encouraging their three children to do the right thing and supporting the children as they each gained college degrees. John Lewis had a strong family and loving father who set a positive example. Charles and Medgar Evers had strong family support even as they each had to pursue their education under difficult circumstances. They observed their father refuse to adhere to the Mississippi custom requiring blacks to step off the sidewalk as whites approached. Little wonder his sons confronted the social ills of the south so directly and passionately.

Family is not confined to just mother and father. The black culture must develop the dictum that every black child, whether supported by a strong black family, is our responsibility to support, to encourage, to love. We must meet each child or adult with a smile, with a "How are you doing today?" as we walk the street and meet each other. As I have questioned how a white family could watch a lynching of a black man, I also must question how a black youth in Chicago or Baltimore could kill a black member of his black family extended. We are all one family!

There is always an uproar in our community when an unarmed black male is killed by a policeman. Each incident must be investigated to its fullest extent. Yet, there is another option available to our community that would stop these deaths and keep our children safe. Better parenting is that option. It is the responsibility of each parent to protect their children, to keep them out of harm's way, to reinforce the concept of "good behavior," honesty, and self-worth. The prisons are filled by black men and women. Why is even one black person there? They are there because the black family failed them, because each child was not wrapped in our protective cultural blanket and because each child was not taught that he or she must always exhibit the best ideals of our rich culture. Yes! Martin Luther King went to jail, John Lewis went to jail, James Lawson went to prison, but their brave acts were in support of each of us. They were products of strong black families and their sacrifices reflect that. There was an instruction given me by my mother that I've never forgotten. A black child moved to our neighborhood who immediately became my playmate. Her instruction was, "Until we get to know him better, when he enters a store, you stay outside. When he exits, you can go in." The arrangement didn't last long since he had good manners and was a positive playmate.

## EDUCATION

My Jewish friend, Edward Jasnow, tells of a conversation he had with an elementary school friend.

> Ed: "Where do you think you will go to college?"
>
> Friend: "I'm not going to college. I will join my dad's union!"
>
> Ed: "Wait! You have to go to college!"
>
> Friend: "No I don't."

Ed rushes home and says to his mother: "I thought you said that college was mandatory."

Mother: "I said it was mandatory for you."

My point is that other competing cultures place almost a universal requirement for higher education on their children. This is not so in many parts of the black society.

I will focus on two issues regarding the education of black children and young adults that are not usually part of the discussion. The first issue is the responsibility to create a nurturing school environment that also maintains high academic standards for each student from 1st grade to college or trade school graduation. When public schools are not capable of meeting this standard, the black community will be required to support private/Christian schools that meet the educational standards. This model is in place at St. Francis High School in Newark, NJ, which has been highlighted on *60 Minutes*. There are other similar initiatives across the country that could be replicated on a national scale. A second example is occurring at HBCU Universities, particularly at Virginia State University, where incoming students are assigned a Big Brother or Big Sister.

The second issue is the hidden impact of RACIAL ASSIGNMENT within our society. Without a doubt, prejudice and stereo types exist in our society. Blacks in our country, as well as Jews in Germany in the 1930s, faced prejudices designating them as inferior. For one, it is my opinion that these prejudices impact the black community throughout an individual's life particularly as regards opportunity. Second, it is my opinion that "do good" or government assistance programs simply perpetuate the prejudicial stereotypes of Black Americans. The two programs, in my mind, that contribute to this perpetuation are (1) government assistance programs like Minority Business Set-Aside Programs, and (2) the over 150 years existence of historically black colleges and universities. No doubt! These fine institutions make tremendous contribution to the education of our children. BUT WHAT IS THE LONG TERM COST? I pose the following questions to these programs.

- Do they perpetuate the stereotype of black inferiority?

- Do they make us a permanent minority?

- Does help foster or hinder competitive business practices?

- Blacks have matured, become competitive today. Do we really need help?

Dr. Michael Lomax, President and CEO of UNCF, has identified six reasons supporting the relevance of HBCU's.

- Low Cost; Best Buy

- Meets needs of low-income

- Low cost narrows the racial wealth gap

- Campus climate fosters success

- Supports unemployment and under employment

- HBCU's offer true value

Due to the two competing realities, I would suggest two reasonable options. First, HBCU's should recruit students of all races becoming socially and ethically mixed. Second, minority businesses accepted into the program must exhibit skills and business histories that will guarantee absorption into the normal competitive marketplace. During my professional career, I have taught students at the HBCU University of Arkansas, Pine Bluff campus, and have recruited students from three HBCU's at Howard, Atlanta and Florida A&M Universities. Further, I have managed a federal government contracting office that managed the work of large numbers of black firms who entered through the set-aside programs.

## POLITICAL POWER

The black culture must demand that every adult person assume the duty of voting in each and every election. I cringe at the thought of voter registration drives for black citizens. We have used these drives in the past, but no more. If you are black, if you are young or old, if you have means or if you are poor, your obligation to your black culture as long as you live is to vote in every federal, state, or local election. Once again, I turn to our strengthened culture. The vote obligation not only rests with the individual, but also rests with the culture supports (education, transportation, funding) that will support the individual initiative. If you are black, your responsibility to your culture is to vote. Period!

## FINANCIAL STRENGTH

While I am not an expert in this area, I do know that we must, as a culture, husband our financial posture in a variety of initiatives (banking, nonprofits, educational supports, accumulation of family assets) that mimics the achievements of the other ethnic groups presented herein.

## GRIT

What has gotten us this far in this United States of America? From our slave days (see Robert Smalls) from our Jim Crow days (see our Buffalo Soldiers), from the Civil Rights Era (see the domestic workers walking for 381 days), we as a people have overcome so much through our individual grit. Grit has been the primary foundation of our culture, and it must be sustained as an integral part as we move into tomorrow.

After our look at today, what strategies must we be cognizant of in order to move forward successfully. These strategies are what I will refer to as the Admonitions.

## DISCARD OLD, OUTDATED LEADERSHIP

Our new leadership must come from the financial and political world. Ministers, lawyers, and Activists who have brought us this far must play a more supportive role to the new leadership styles that are efficacious, that bring sustainable change and results affecting all in our culture

The political ranks are being filled in Federal, State and Local elections by highly qualified black candidates. There already has been elected a bicultural president in Barack Obama; Stacey Abrams may become the first black woman governor, and numerous blacks are serving as United States senators and representatives in our Federal government. The business ranks are being filled by risk-taking black entrepreneurs like Kenneth C. Frazier, Chief Executive of Merck and Company (one of the largest pharmaceutical companies in the world).

In her excellent book, *White Rage*, Carol Anderson, Ph.D. gives a thorough accounting of the successful dismantling of black progress through the constructed barriers. Her chapters are entitled:

> *Reconstructing Reconstruction*
> *Derailing the Great Migration*
> *Burning Brown to the Ground*
> *Rolling Back Civil Rights*
> *How to Unelect a Black President*

By relying on the well-meaning efforts of ministers, lawyers, and activists, the above listed negative results were inevitable. Today on August 5, 2018,

Reverend Al Sharpton stated his desire on national TV to join protesters in Tampa, FL, over the death of an unarmed black man. The man was killed by a white man operating under the Florida "Right to Carry" Law. Oh Boy! Another march; another step backwards! There was another alternative:

- The black man could have been wrapped in "Our Culture Blanket" that made him aware of his positive self-worth. No need to start the confrontation over a parking space.

- Our culture also could have made this black man cognizant of the white fear that has gripped their community as the country turns majority of color.

- Al Sharpton must pivot away from fights and marches that are not in our interests. Voting, education, personal achievement, and pride in being black and caring for our family are our new means of protests. What specifically has marching accomplished?

## DISCARD CIVIL RIGHTS

As with the old leadership, the Civil Rights Movement got us where we are today, but its usefulness as a foundation for our absorption into the new bicultural society is not of any help. Don't you doubters get it?! As of today, blacks are now an integral, necessary component of the new bicultural, biracial society. If you have brown skin, you are no longer different. If you have an Asian appearance, your unique features blend smoothly with the others who are unique in their own way. If you go to a bank money dispensing machine and only speak Spanish, it will give you the Spanish Speaking option. If you have white skin and no longer have white privilege, you are free to enjoy your accomplishments on the merits of your hard work.

Immigrants arrived seeking opportunity not civil rights. We can be the leaders in our new society. We have the skill sets, the grit, the necessary understandings resulting from experiences gained from being on the bottom. To continue to focusing on civil rights, is to succumb to "their" assignment of us as inferior, as needing help (Brown vs. Board), of needing special treatment (minority business set-a-sides, HBCUs). We must recognize that we are as prepared as any white or other ethnic group to lead this nation. Through a major improvement in our culture, through a new pivot emphasizing "opportunity focus" and through "hard work," we need not ask for civil rights.

## ASSIMILATION

Evidence has been presented that immigrant groups arriving on our shores have managed their assimilation into the United States society. The word "managed" has been used to depict the process by which each immigrant group used their unique culture strengths (e.g., political, financial, educational) to achieve assimilation. Evidence has been presented that George Washington himself encouraged arriving Germans to adapt to the English cultured of the new nation. It is, therefore, evident that assimilation has been an important ingredient that supported the successful establishment of our "diverse human platform."

The road to assimilation for Black Americans, however, has not been as decisive as for the other immigrant groups. For one, blacks did not possess the strong culture base as the other immigrants did. Second, many centuries of slavery presented no opportunity for assimilation. Further, there is a third obstacle today inhibiting black assimilation. Internal black resistance particularly in the black middle and lower class. Some contributing factors are (1) a desire to retain African heritage visibly, socially, and emotionally, (2) a lack of understanding of the complexity of assimilation by definition, and (3) a dislike of brothers and sisters who appear (by speech, dress, education) to have become "white."

We must start with an understanding of what assimilation truly is. It is one word that has been used to inaccurately describe a complex social process. We can break it down with the following definitions:

**Acculturation** - the culture system of one group replaces the traditional practices and beliefs of another group often after conquest and subjugation.

**Assimilation** - the process by which individuals or groups of different ethnic heritage are absorbed into the dominate culture of a society.

**Cultural Assimilation** - the process by which a person or group's language or culture comes to resemble those of another group.

**Full Assimilation** - occurs when new members become indistinguishable from members of the other group.

**Amalgamation** - refers to the blending of cultures rather than one group mixing itself into another.

It is the opinion of this writer that blacks should consider amalgamation/assimilation as a positive step. As you can see from the definitions presented, there is no set prescription. The options available are multiple that one may choose to fit into her or his preference and chosen life style. It is further my opinion that amalgamation/assimilation is an unavoidable option if one lives in the United States. Not only is it unavoidable but it can "creep into our life" without offering you a choice. Gentrification of your all black neighborhood, marriage outside your race, white friendships gained at work or social events are real life occurrences that foster amalgamation/assimilation.

The fact is that blacks cannot ignore the benefits accruing to our competitor ethnic groups who have assimilated. The fact is that 30 to 50 percent of blacks have accepted assimilation already. The fact is that assimilation does not require you to abandon your culture. You carry your culture with you only and proudly with a prospect of infusing their culture with your beautiful culture.

## DISPENSE WITH VICTIM MENTALITY

Whenever I discuss Black American circumstances with other blacks, the first response is immediately focused on "what white people did to us, slavery, lynchings, rapes." I believe a more positive discussion would center first on the improvements that must be made to our culture and then on historical experiences, both positive and negative, that can be used to target improvement options. The Japanese culture trait, Darma (do not complain), needs to be incorporated into black culture.

## OPPORTUNITY FOR ALL - THE NEW CULTURE

It is obvious that our black society has (since Emancipation) not set a standard of opportunity for all blacks. From the start, DuBois and Washington spoke of the talented 10 percent. While possibly unintended, they assigned the uneducated 90 percent of their brothers and sisters to the bottom of our society. Today, the initial assignment is a fixture in our culture. Yes! The marches, the law suits, the legislations, even the nonviolent confrontation strategies have propelled the 10 percent to a possible 40 percent of our population. That being said, it still leaves a percentage of our community as an underclass. There can be no room in our society for a talented elite. The rich must embrace the poor. The educated must devise schemes to ensure that all are educated. All must be moving forward, not necessarily at the same pace, but forward nonetheless.

In the previously mentioned interview with Charles Evers at his radio station in Jackson, MS, I asked him what were his thoughts on what our priorities should be. Here is a man whose brother was assassinated, who had to walk 10 miles to school each day, and who was subject to the daily humiliations during his youth. To my surprise, Charles said our efforts should be directed to Chicago, where the black-on-black murder rate is killing our children. Charles, in his wisdom and to his eternal credit, was focused on the improvements needed in our own society. To gain a personal appreciation, I walked from Decatur to Newton after interviewing Charles in Jackson. My school distance in Elkland was a quarter-mile.

## THE CIVIL RIGHTS LEGACY

"Researchers at the Pew Research Center have declared that Asian Americans achievement represents... major milestones of economic success and social assimilation in the United States." Further research found that they enjoyed "shared economic mobility and high education rates

and collectively value cultural traits such as the importance of family, respect for elders, and a pervasive belief in the rewards of hard work." (*The Making of Asian America*, Erika Lee)

Immigrant Asians (as above) focus on (1) economic success, (2) social assimilation, (3) economic mobility, (4) high education rates, and (5) value culture traits like the importance family, respect for elders, and pervasive belief in rewards of hard work. Even if given a pass on the purpose and courage of the past struggles, the black culture has not included a holistic social focus on family respect for elders and belief in rewards for hard work.

I view the Modern Civil Rights Era to be a short-term tactical success against entrenched national resistances. I am amazed every day of my life at the courage and selfless desire for change displayed by the activists in the movement. While I was developing my own youthful challenges during this same period, I know that I could not have been a participant in the nonviolent protests of John Lewis or Jim Zwerg and their associates. I believe that there were two distinct results from the actions of the period. The first is that many improvement targets are fixed improvements such as fair housing. The second is that most fixes did not help the disenfranchised. For instance, if you were an educated black, fair housing provides one an opportunity to acquire any home in any neighborhood. If you are a poor minority, the previous restriction, applicable to you, still applies.

There are numerous improvements necessary as time progresses:

**Family** - How often is family discussed in literature during the era? Only 38 percent of black children under 18 live with two parents. In his book, *Reckoning with Race*, Gene Dattel writes, "The Family is the first incubator of behavioral norms that foster education, hard work and citizenship." He further cites the shortcomings of the black "Many Rivers to Cross Festival" held in Atlanta in October 2016. The three themes were (1) voting, (2) mass incarceration, and (3) police and community relations. Nothing was highlighted regarding (1) education, (2) family, (3) employment, or (4) black-on-black crime.

**Assimilation** - While the founding fathers left black citizenship out of the Constitution, they understood that assimilation of the arriving immigrants was a necessity for a cohesive union. George Washington in 1793 urged arriving Germans to "intermix with our citizens and assimilate."

**Education** - Jason Riley in his book, *Please Stop Helping Us*, addresses the liberal attempts to help black people. He discusses the failed liberal attempts in many areas, and especially notes the weakness of our black culture. He shows a report that the reading scores of black boys in 8th grade to be barely higher than the scores of white girls in 4th grade.

**Culture** - Strength of culture and reliance on your culture in order to navigate the complex and challenging world has proven to be the protective antidote for individuals. There are certain mandatory requirements to be judged a contributing member of the black culture. At a minimum:

Vote - dispense with voter drives

Maximize education for yourself and others

Maintain vigorous family support

Assist the less fortunate in your culture

Work collectively with all other culture members

## BLACK CULTURE SCORECARD

### A. Collectivism Nonexistent
- Colin Kaepernick – Quarterback – San Francisco 49ers
- Tommie Smith – Black Power Salute – 1968 Olympics
- John Carlos - Black Power Salute – 1968 Olympics

### B. Collaborators or Independents
- Clarence Thomas – Associate Justice of the US Supreme Court
- Ben Carson – US Secretary of Housing and Urban Development
- Tim Scott – US Senator – South Carolina

# 11

# WHITE PRIVILEGE
# TO WHITE MALAISE

## INTRODUCTION

The previous chapter addressed the Black American culture and the black social structure as a whole. The chapter took a critical look at the culture weaknesses while offering recommendations on how to make the culture stronger and be better prepared for tomorrow. It is the purpose of this chapter to take a similar approach in an analysis of White America. Does White America have a culture? Can you identify white culture by its working class culture? Will White America try to maintain its whiteness or white privileges as they are being attacked and diminished by our emerging bicultural society? Can the white working class pivot from its malaise of today and return to the strong cultures displayed by their immigrant ancestors? This chapter is providing a warning to the white working class. The elephant in the room is the dominance and flexibility of the business community combined with the government and the oligarchy. They have begun their pivot away from white privilege towards the bicultural community. When I was young, there were no blacks or other minorities in television advertisements. Now the bicultural community is represented in most, if not all, commercials. Their customers are the bicultural society of America!

## THE BEGINNING OF WHITENESS

In 1893, an Australian academic named Charles Henry Pearson predicted in his book, *National Life and Character! A Forecast*, that "White men would be elbowed and hustled, and perhaps even thrust aside by the black and yellow races."

This information was included in a New York Times article entitled, "The Religion of Whiteness Becomes a Suicide Cult," written by Pekaj Mishra dated September 2, 2018. Mr. Mishra further explained that Pearson was prone to believe in the "terrors of racial extensions" due to Australia's geographic location in an Asian neighborhood. Pearson further thought that Australia would have to be the last part of the world where the "higher races" could defend against these lower races. It is important to note that Theodore Roosevelt, Woodrow Wilson, and Donald Trump shared these fears of what evolved into a commonly use phrase of "racial suicide" in today's descriptive language.

In 1897, Theodore Roosevelt complimented Pearson on how well his words were received by "all men here in Washington." Woodrow Wilson, as president, worked to preserve "white civilization and its domination of the planet" at the World War I Paris Peace Conference by denying a racial equality clause in the Covenant of the League of Nations proposed by his wartime ally Japan. Continuing this presidential focus in a 2017 speech, President Trump stated that "the fundamental question of our time is whether the West has the will to survive." These words were fully supported by conservatives. President Trump has continued to support the "White Australia" policies restricting "colored" immigration by its Prime Minister Malcolm Turnbull. In the same New York Times article, Mr. Mishra relates a January 2017 conversation between Trump and Turnbull where Trump agrees with Turnbull's brutal immigration policies saying, "That is a good idea. We should do that, too," referring to Turnbull's desired tactic of locking up refugees on remote islands. It is important to note that Mr. Mishra concludes in his article that the impacts of global migration and the ascendance of the yellow and black and Muslim races will inevitably lead to "race suicide" of the higher races. This struggle to hold on to what they have, he also concludes, will create such a chaos that life on our planet could end.

It is interesting that the noted Black American writer, James Baldwin, has reached a similar conclusion. He writes of the terrible possibility that, "The rulers of the higher races struggling to hold on to what they have stolen from their captives...will precipitate a chaos throughout which, if it does not bring life on this planet to end, will bring about a racial war such as the world has never seen." I find these similar predictions to be without historical relevance based on the evidence presented throughout this book about the resilience of the human experiences since homo sapiens populated the earth.

## THE TROUBLE WITH WHITENESS - PRIVILEGE

I understand that it may not be unfair to discuss the people impacted by privilege, described by Joan C. Williams in her book, *White Working Class*, in this book discussing the cultures of immigrants coming to the United States. The best I can do is describe these people and direct descendants of immigrants and their culture.

As a starting point, it will help if we conduct a review of our immigrant history. Every group, except the initial English settlers, were subject to considerable hardships and barriers. It is further important to note that a common trait shared by each group was hard work, little complaining and adaptability. The Irish Catholics, considered Celts and inside-out blacks, overcame the imposed barriers. The Japanese Bisho family came to Los Angeles after a five-year working journey from Vancouver, Canada, bearing the loss of a daughter in Seattle. The Chinese Chen family escaped China through harrowing trips wherein many perished to settle in New York's Chinatown and early, demeaning work. The Mexican family whose eight children each had to work at the age of 12 to help support the family. The Black

Americans who overcame slavery and extraordinary prejudice to establish themselves as citizens.

These immigrants and the others previously identified were not afraid of taking tremendous risks, were not afraid of hard and dangerous work, were not reticent to pursue work wherever it was available and were willing to be separated from family and associates for long periods of time. While these various immigrant groups have established a similar pattern towards success (through collective support, educational achievement, grit, political, and economic acumen), the white working class displays none of these attributes. Further, they have willfully discarded the positive attributes of their immigrant grandparents.

First, what is the white working class? The best description is provided by Ms. Williams in the above described book. She describes the working class as above the bottom 30 percent and below the top 20 percent of income. This leaves the roughly 50 percent middle class earning between $41,000 to roughly $130,000 in annual income as the working class. Second, and more important, she discusses the social characteristics of this group through a number of revealing chapter titles and analysis. Some of them are as follows:

*Why Doesn't the Working Class Just Move to Where the Jobs Are?*

*Why Doesn't the Working Class Get with It and Go to College?*

*Why Don't They Push Their Kids Harder to Succeed?*

*Don't They Understand that Manufacturing Jobs Aren't Coming Back?*

*Why Don't Working Class Men Just Take Pink Collar Jobs?*

In her Chapter 5, "Why Not Move to Where the Jobs Are?", she provides an articulate analysis supporting their thinking. Here, she discusses the power of "clique networks where everybody knows everyone else and ties run deep." She describes a situation where a Harvard grad (which she is) could easily pick up and accept a position in Silicon Valley when it is where working class children would have a hard time leaving one's support network of family and friends to move away from them. Ms. Williams' point is well-grounded, but her analysis misses an important point.

It is my opinion that the white working class, in their current position, in their current malaise, must adopt the immigrant energies of risk taking of their ancestors. Further, they must mimic the cultural strengths articulated in this book (education emphasis, financial and political strength, family support) that propelled the various immigrants to success.

## THE MATURING OF HYPOCRISY - GASLIGHTING

In her book, *The Origins of Totalitarianism*, Hannah Arendt, a Jewish escapee from Nazi Germany, wrote, "In an ever-changing, incomprehensible world, the masses had reached the point where they would, at the same time, believe everything and nothing, think that everything was possible and nothing was true. Repeated, simplified and false-story lines, which blame scapegoats and offer easy solutions, are preferred over deeper analysis leading to informed opinions."

Gaslighting is a form of psychological manipulation that seeks to sow doubt in a targeted individual or group making them question their own memory, perception, sanity. Gaslighting, at its core, is a form of emotional abuse that slowly eats away at your ability to make judgments. Mrs. Arendt further predicted the precise use of gaslighting that Trump would apply as president. To be effective, "the ruling class must forge an alliance between capital and the mob." The mob being the marginalized whites who will gain elevation above the non-whites he has attacked.

If the reader will refer to the Chapter 8 and the discussion of hypocrisy, you will find it quite similar to gaslighting. Aimé Césaire's discussion on hypocrisy cited it as incapable of solving problems yet so odious that it is not likely to deceive. I capture a significant difference in hypocrisy's sister gaslighting. Gaslighting may not be recognized by its recipient and has a more psychologically, manipulative purpose. While on vacation at a resort location, I conversed with several highly educated white couples who were obviously well-to-do couples this summer. While I expected at least some to lean towards traditional conservative values, I was shocked that they all supported President Trump's nativist policies. Césaire's observation that hypocrisy is so easily identifiable due to its odious, repulsive nature, the same cannot be said of the reach of gaslighting. Trump's gaslighting attacks (e.g. (1) Russia's attack on our electoral system should be dismissed; (2) that thousands of people cheered the 9/11 attack in New Jersey; (3) that the CIA and FBI cannot be believed; (4) that the United States is the highest-taxed nation; and (5) that crime is rising when it is actually falling) are against our institutions not just his election comments against Mexican and immigrants.

We should be aware, but not worried about this latest iteration of nativism. Trump is just the continuation of nativism sentiment carried out by some of our most beloved presidents. President Franklin Roosevelt denied the entry of 900 Jewish refugees escaping Hitler while on a ship in New York Harbor. They returned to Germany to known fate. His relative, while in his government, refused the entry of 20,000 Jewish children, saying that they would produce another 20,000 ugly Jewish children. The Legislative Acts such as the Chinese Exclusion Act, the 1924 Immigration Act excluding Japanese and Italian/Central European immigrants, and the California Law restricting ownership or leasing of land by naturalized Japanese are part of our past. The nativist result that Trump is attempting will fail, as all previous nativist attempts did fail. This country should manage migration not immigration.

White males are the terrorists in our society. They have always been! In the United States, there has been terror imposed on slaves and new immigrants. After slavery was abolished, there was rape, lynching, sharecropping, and Black Codes by which terror was imposed. Today, more often than not, white males are the perpetrators of mass murders in our schools and universities, at our entertainment venues, on our streets through "open carry" laws and on our public institutions and politicians. We know that FEAR is a natural human instinct. Fear protects us from predators. In my opinion, "white fear" is the primary stimulant for the malaise. Overcome your fears through hard work like your ancestors.

Fortunately, it is a small and vicious segment of the white population occupying the "hard right" of our political spectrum that fosters and executes the inhumane acts. These vicious acts are further supported by state legislative acts opposing gun control and voting rights of minorities. Reflecting on this carnage brings a certain sadness to my mind. I think of the vast majority of whites who chose to live by the positive ideals that are available to all who live here. I am sad when I think of all the white males and females who strive in their daily lives to love and honor all people whether rich or poor, whether immigrant or minority. I am sad when I recall the sacrifices of Jim Zwerg or Rita Bender and Mickey Schwerner who place themselves in harm's way for the benefit of black citizens. Yet I particularly feel sad for those captured by the hypocritical pronouncements of their leaders on the right. I bring this observation from a position of understanding. In my own black culture, there are worrying trends and beliefs that do not sit well with me. There are Black Nationalists as well as the Nation of Islam, headed by Minister Louis Farrakhan. The NOI is an African American political and religious organization whose goal is to improve the spiritual, mental, social, and economic conditions of African Americans. Yet, while they desire separation and espouse hatred of Jews, I find no overt, harmful, destructive acts as part of their agenda. As a Black American, I am proud to be in the company of NOI members as they are mannerly and well dressed in suits and bow ties. Quite the opposite of the Charlottesville far right hoodlums.

**MALAISE:** A condition that harms or weakens a society or group as well as a vague sense of mental or moral ill-being.

It is this condition, the moral disfunction of the hard right, consisting of at least two elements… the political nationalism and the Christian nationalism that is dangerous. It is led by an immoral leader who preaches hate from the White House with Christian nationalist leaders leading Bible study groups in the

White House attended by cabinet members. In her New York Times Article, "Why Trump Reigns as King Cyrus," dated January 1, 2019, Katherine Stewart writes, "This isn't the religious right we thought we knew. The Christian nationalists movement today is authoritarian, paranoid and patriarchal at its core. They aren't fighting a culture war. They're making a direct attack on democracy itself."

# 12

# THE LAST MINORITY

This book is about the contributions made by immigrants and their accompanying cultures towards the development of America. The story is told through the lives of two black youths who came to their maturity during the modern civil rights era. The civil rights era, however, is but one subset of the many unique and similar immigrant experiences of Jews, of Irish Catholics, of Eastern Europeans, of Asians, of Hispanics. Over a period exceeding two centuries, those arriving cultures have transformed America from a single (white relevant) society. Many of the old power structure events (e.g., states' rights, voter suppression advocates) still are actively trying to maintain white power. That is a fool's errand! The real strategy of the triumvirate (oligarchs, business, government) is to retain that power and position. The oligarchs recognize that their membership is now comprised of multi-millionaire people of color and different ethnicities. Minority businessmen are the heads of major corporations.

It is important to note that the immigrant groups came with strong cultures, and they successfully overcame the barriers (social and legal) imposed. The slaves, on the other hand, did not arrive with a cohesive culture. Once free, however, the Black American culture is a work in progress. Some of our culture elements are strong like Mendel's and John's family support. Conversely, family structure in our overall culture is very weak for many.

ASSIMILATION was the first step of the evolutionary transformation of America's society. The Irish and Jewish immigrants have described it in the cited literature. Cultural assimilation did not have a significant impact on the white standards since immigrant cultures came to absorb the elements of the dominant white culture. The years of cultural assimilation provided me with a relaxed comfort in displaying my own culture's nuances (e.g., black language, black rhythm, subtle arrogance, physical attributes). Incorporating the strength of family love and other culture strengths made the move to CULTURAL ACCOMMODATION, a natural progression for me and other blacks. Accommodation is the public display of both the host culture and the individual's original culture. CULTURAL AMALGAMATION, where our American culture is now, results from blending together two or more cultures creating a new culture. This amalgamation was confirmed with the election of Barak Obama. He is not the first black president! He is the first multicultural president. This amalgamation is confirmed when I and my wife of Croatian descent, gather with friends in social settings. There is a magical blending of skin colors, of ascents from Ghana, Argentina, Lebanon, India, China, or Poland. When I gather with my "Black American" friends in an upscale suburb of Washington, DC, I always lament that there are no other ethnics or cultures there. I gain their humorous wrath when I remind them that they are the new privileged, socially closer to the oligarchs than the undereducated, underemployed black brothers and sisters residing a few miles away in lower class circumstances.

The new American society is peopled by OLIGARCHS of many colors and ethnicities. One of them, Obama, is a Harvard Law graduate, his wife is a Harvard Law graduate, his older daughter attends Harvard University and attended elite private schools. If there are prerogatives to be bestowed, they will be reserved for those Americans of any color or any ethnicity who meet the class standard of finance, of education, of political awareness. These people are the PRODUCERS, they make our trains run, they run our governments, they send our astronauts to space. The remaining citizens who are poor, who are undereducated, who refuse to assimilate and who refuse to adjust their life styles in the face of certain change will become EXPLOITED.

The EXPLOITED are now of any color or ethnicity, including the whites, now without privilege. Do not forget the dictum of six centuries ago that laborers should be kept "at the margins of subsistence." The last minority has been identified. The last minority has been assigned!

# EPILOGUE

## 2018 - SPRING IN AMERICA - REVISITED

Mendel and John are now approaching their 80th birthdays. Each, in his own way, sought to "take part in the actions and passions off their time." We were introduced to Mendel and John in April 1961 as they embarked on their adult journeys. From the beginning, John's life was conducted on a national scale. He embarked on the mission confronting racial prejudice while in college as a teenager. He met with the President of the United States during a national crisis when he was just 23 years old. He was one of the 13 speakers at the 1963 March on Washington where Dr. Martin Luther King, Jr., gave his famous "I have a Dream Speech." He became recognized as a national leader as a Congressman from Georgia where he serves today. Mendel, John's unknown partner, likewise sought the actions in life through the extremes related to military service, through a career supporting numerous federal programs involving NASA and health issues while overcoming physical limitations throughout.

Today, there is a new reality confronting both Mendel and John. An article in the New York Times "The Rise of Black Progressives," dated September 6, 2018, highlights this new reality. During a recent Democratic Primary in Massachusetts, a white, liberal Congressman (Michael Capuano) was being challenged by a black, Progressive (Ayanna Presley). Representative Capuano was supposed throughout the Primary by two significant black politicians, Congressman John Lewis and former Governor Deval Patrick.

*Congrssman John Lewis and Mendel Hill, 2015*

While I have no firsthand information regarding why John and Deval supported the white liberal over the black progressive, I can say that I probably would have made the same decision. Over the past six decades, I have established and maintained close, professional relationships with whites. While working at a national bank in Washington, DC, in 1981, another employee asked for a copy of my resume. A week later, I received a call from the governor's office in California scheduling an interview. The interview resulted in my being hired as the Executive Director of the $300M Century Freeway Housing Construction Program in Los Angeles. The position required an appointment by Governor Jerry Brown and confirmation by the California Senate. In 1983, after being fired by the new Governor, a dear friend secured a position for me at the California Institute of Technology (Caltech) in Pasadena, CA, which led to my appointment as the first business manager for the International Space Station Project in 1987 for NASA. The fellow employee at the National Bank was a young white lady named Marcy

Kaptur, who subsequently became the longest serving Congresswoman in Congress. The dear friend of 52 years at Caltech University was a Jewish man, Edward Jasnow.

John and I have spent the past six decades establishing commitments that we must honor. The young progressives combined with the newly elected women and men of Congress have to establish their own template for action and progress. Do not attack wealthy and "the system"; impose your will on the system through the basics of voting, economic boycotts, unshakeable coalitions. Do not champion "free rides" of education or economic equality. Our history and growth is based on hard work, on grit. Instead of free college, the goal can be "college without debt." Service through civic organizations or the military can be productive, acceptable alternatives. Replace Congressional Acts with state and local actions and laws. Stacey Abrams and Andrew Gillum represent the most likely opportunity for success.